EVENTS MANAGEMENT

DR. Raj Kumar Singh
D.H.C.T. Mgmt. (W.B.)
P.G.D.B. Mgmt. (U.P.)
C.F.N. (Delhi)
MHCIMA (London)
Ph.D. (Management)
Director
'SAMS' Institute of Hotel Management,
Varanasi

AMAN PUBLICATIONS
NEW DELHI (INDIA)

Published by
Rajiv Jain for Aman Publications
LG-4A, Ganpati Bhawan,
4675-B/21, Ansari Road,
Darya Ganj, Delhi - 110002
PH: 23255012, 23282127
E-mail: sshjbs@yahoo.com

First Edition 2014
ISBN-81-8204-032-9 (HB)

SOLE DISTRIBUTOR
JINDAL BOOK SERVICES
LG-4A, Ganpati Bhawan,
4675-B/21, Ansari Road,
Darya Ganj, Delhi - 110002

Laser Typesetting by:
S.M. Graphics, Delhi,

Printed by:
Indraprastha Press , Delhi, India

PREFACE

Since the time immemorial, human beings have found ways to mark important events in their lives. Both in private and in public, they felt the need to mark important occasions in their lives and to celebrates the key moments. Today events are central to our culture as perhaps never before. Increases in leisure time and discretionary spendings have led to a proliferation of public events, celebrations and entertainment. Festivals and special events have grown into a massive industry worldwide, generating billions of dollars for regional centres, states, and countries.

Governments now support and promote events as part of their strategies for economic development, nation-building and destination marketing. Corporations and businesses embrace events as key elements in their marketing strategies and image promotion. The enthusiasm of community groups and individuals for their own interests and passions gives rise to a marvellous array of events on almost every subjects and themes imaginable. The future is bright for event managers equipped with the essential training and skills required to research, plan, schedule, organise, and market special events anywhere in the world.

This book is an integrated guide on how to start, develop, and manage profitable special events. It provides comprehensive information on the theory and procedures

Preface

CONTENTS

1

Categories of Planned Special Events

A planned special event impacts the transportation system by generating an increase in travel demand in addition to possibly causing a reduction in roadway capacity because of event staging. The first step toward achieving an accurate prediction of event-generated travel demand and potential transportation system capacity constraints involves gaining an understanding of the event characteristics and how these characteristics affect transportation operations.

In turn, practitioners can classify the planned special event in order to draw comparisons between the subject event and similar historical events to shape travel forecasts and gauge transportation impacts. Figure 1 shows typical operational characteristics of a planned special event. Each characteristic represents a variable that greatly influences the scope of event operation and its potential impact on the transportation system. These variables include:

— Event time of occurrence defines the time of day(s) the event is open for business, a key variable when comparing event-generated traffic to background traffic. For example, weekday events may face

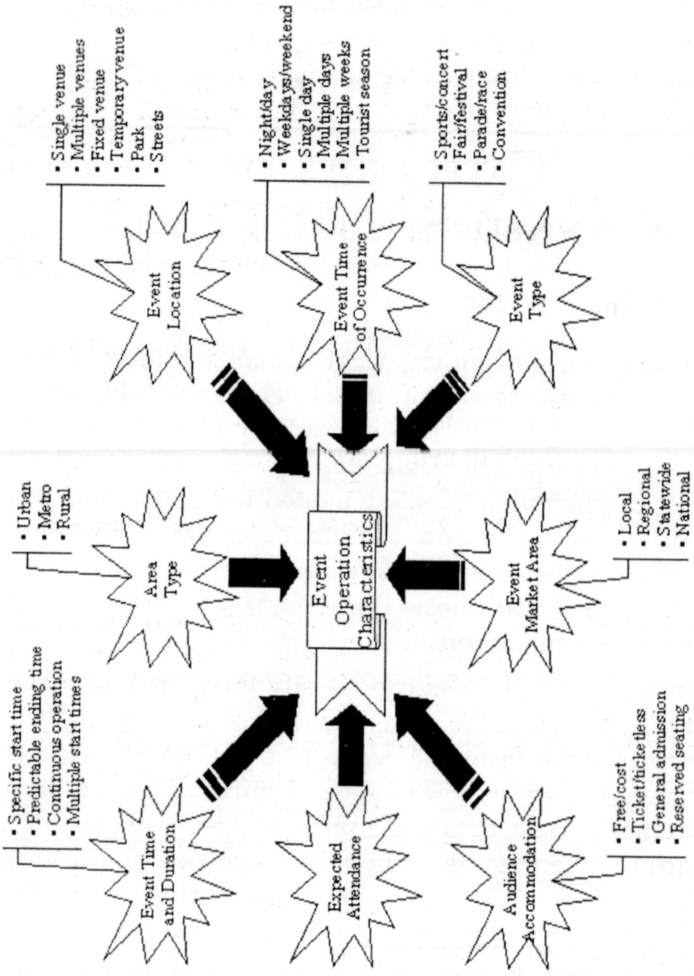

Figure 1. Event Operation Characteristics

constraints on roadway, transit, and parking capacity because of commuter travel.

— Event time and duration defines whether the event features a specific main event start time, likely to condense event patron arrival, or operates continuously throughout the day where patrons may freely come and go.

— Event location defines the characteristics of the venue(s) location and connection to the existing transportation infrastructure.

  a) Typically, fixed venues, such as stadiums or arenas, feature high-capacity parking areas adjacent to the venue and good access to/from adjacent freeways and principal arterial streets.

  b) Temporary venues may lack these features, thus requiring the development of a detailed site access and parking plan.

— Area type defines the scope of available transportation services, the characteristics of background traffic traversing the area, and the various stakeholders that may become involved in event planning and management. These characteristics influence the event operations planning process and day-of-event travel management, yet significantly vary across rural, urban, and metropolitan areas.

— Event market area defines the area from where event patrons originate and the scope of event exposure.

  a) Political conventions or major industry exhibitions feature a national scope where the majority of attendees do not reside in the host city.

— Expected attendance defines the maximum, estimated number of event patrons.

  a) Attendance estimates may include the anticipated number of VIPs, advance ticket holders, patrons with an assigned parking pass, and patrons requiring special assistance.

b) With regard to sporting events, key components in estimating attendance involve home team performance and visiting team attraction.

c) Games involving high-profile visiting teams or performers may sell-out far in advance of the event, allowing stakeholders sufficient notice to take appropriate measures.

d) Attendance impacts traffic operations in the immediate vicinity of the event venue depending on the access and parking capacity furnished at the venue.

— Audience accommodation defines the potential to predict the number and origins of event-generated trips in addition to the type of trip patrons may make to the venue.

a) Attendance at free events is hard to predict and may vary considerably based on weather conditions and other factors on the day-of-event.

b) Events featuring advance ticket sales and reserved seating may decrease the number of event patrons making a spur-of-the-moment decision to attend an event.

— Event type defines the type of event that may be subject to special regulations and permit requirements. The event type includes many of the previously defined characteristics of planned special events that influence event-generated travel demand and level of impact on the transportation system. Event planners may refer to event type when researching impacts on travel caused by similar events.

Types of Planned Special Events

There are five categories of planned special events, which were:

- Discrete/recurring event at a permanent venue
- Continuous event
- Street use event
- Regional/multi-venue event
- Rural event

Table 1 contrasts some general characteristics specific to each defined event category.

Table 1. Characteristics of Different Planned Special Event Categories

Characteristic	Planned Special Event Category
	Discrete/Recurring Event at a Permanent Venue
Event Location	Fixed venue
Event Time of Occurrence	Single day; Night/day; Weekday/weekend
Event Time and Duration	Specific start time; Predictable ending time
Area Type	Metro; Urban
Event Market Area	Local; Regional; Statewide; National
Expected Audience	Known venue capacity
Audience Accommodation	Cost; Ticket; Reserved seating; General admission
Event Type	Sporting and concert events at stadiums, arenas, and amphitheaters.
	Continuous Event
Characteristic	Planned Special Event Category
Event Location	Temporary venue; Park; Fixed venue
Event Time of Occurrence	Single/multiple days; Weekends; Multiple weeks
Event Time and Duration	Continuous operation

Area Type	Metro; Urban
Event Market Area	Local; Regional
Expected Audience	Capacity of venue not always known
Audience Accommodation	Free/cost; Ticket/ticketless; General admission
Event Type	Fairs; Festivals; Conventions/expos; Air/automobile shows

	Street Use Event
Characteristic	Planned Special Event Category
Event Location	Streets
Event Time of Occurrence	Single day; Weekends
Event Time and Duration	Specific start time; Predicable ending time
Area Type	Metro; Urban; Rural
Event Market Area	Local; Regional
Expected Audience	Capacity generally not known
Audience Accommodation	Free; Ticketless
Event Type	Parades; Marathons; Bicycle races; Motorcycle rallies; Grand Prix auto races; Dignitary motorcade

	Regional/Multi-Venue Event
Characteristic	Planned Special Event Category
Event Location	(Multiple) Fixed venue; Temporary venue; Streets
Event Time of Occurrence	Single/multiple days; Weekends
Event Time and Duration	Specific start time; Predictable ending time; Continuous operation
Area Type	Metro (typically); Urban; Rural
Event Market Area	Local; Regional; Statewide; National
Expected Audience	Overall capacity generally not known if continuous events or street use events involved
Audience Accommodation	Free/cost; Ticket/ticketless
Event Type	Sporting games; Fireworks displays; Multiple planned special events within a region that occur at or near the same time

Rural Event	
Characteristic	Planned Special Event Category
Event Location	Fixed venue; Temporary venue; Park
Event Time of Occurrence	Single/multiple days; Weekends; Tourist season
Event Time and Duration	Specific start time; Predictable ending time; Continuous operation
Area Type	Rural
Event Market Area	Local; Regional
Expected Audience	Capacity of venue not always known
Audience Accommodation	Free/cost; Ticket/ticketless
Event Type	Discrete/recurring event; Continuous event

In recognising the unique characteristics of each category of planned special event regarding trip generation and event impact on transportation system operations, many jurisdictions across the country have developed distinct planning processes, policies, and regulations specific to particular event categories. Each of the five defined event categories are briefly described below.

Discrete/Recurring Event at a Permanent Venue

A discrete/recurring event at a permanent venue occurs on a regular basis, and it has a specific starting time and predictable ending time. Events classified under this category have predictable peak arrival and departure rates relative to other categories of planned special events. These events generate high peak travel demand rates because of patron urgency to arrive at the venue by a specific event start time. Moreover, these events end abruptly upon game time expiration or the conclusion of a final song, which creates high peak departure rates. Stadiums and arenas occasionally host weeknight events that may conflict with commuter traffic, especially if media broadcasting the event mandates a specific start time.

Continuous Event

A continuous event occurs over a single or multiple days. Unlike a discrete/recurring event at a permanent venue, continuous events do not exhibit sharp peak arrival and peak departure rates. Event patrons typically arrive and depart throughout the event day. Aside from conventions and state/county fairs, many continuous events take place at a temporary venue, a park, or other large open space. As a result, roadway and parking capacity issues may arise in the immediate area surrounding a temporary venue.

Temporary venues may not have a defined spectator capacity, thus creating uncertainties in forecasting event-generated trips since a "sell-out" cap does not exist.

Street Use Event

A street use event occurs on a street requiring temporary closure. These events generally occur in a city or town central business district; however, race events or motorcycle rallies may necessitate temporary closure of arterial streets or limited-access highways. A street use event significantly impacts businesses and neighbourhoods adjacent to the event site from the perspective of parking and access. A street use event closes a segment(s) of the roadway network and causes background and event traffic to divert onto alternate routes, thus increasing traffic demand on other streets in the roadway network. Filming activities may require the closure of major roadways for an extended duration, but stakeholders can work with production companies on day-of-the-week scheduling.

Regional/Multi-Venue Event

A regional/multi-venue event refers to multiple planned special events that occur within a region at or near the same time. The collection of events may have different starting times and differ in classification category. A number of major metropolitan areas have two or more adjacent fixed venues or venues utilising the same freeway corridor. Multiple venues may occasionally host events on the same day.

Rural Event

Rural events encompass any discrete/recurring event or continuous event occurring in a rural area. Planned special events occurring in rural areas deserve a stand-alone classification category for several reasons:

— Need for stakeholders to assume new and/or expanded roles.

— Existence of limited road capacity to access the event venue and potentially limited parking capacity at the venue.

— Existence of fewer alternate routes to accommodate event and background traffic.

— Lack of regular transit service and hotels near the venue.

— Existence of limited or no permanent infrastructure for monitoring and managing traffic.

Impacts of Planned Special Events

Stakeholders responsible for planning and managing travel for planned special events must gauge the potential severity of a planned special event. Agencies must determine with certainty if a planned special event will affect or impede the normal flow of traffic and if yes, how much impact will the event have. Answers to these questions determine the scope of the transportation management plan required to mitigate event-generated impacts on travel in addition to the number of stakeholders that become involved in advance planning and day-of-event travel management activities.

The stakeholders and resources involved in traffic incident management and managing travel for planned special events overlap. The following examples of classifying a planned special event under a traffic incident severity level illustrate how traffic incident responders determine the resources and level of effort required to manage traffic during a planned special event:

A new chapter included in the proposed amendments to the 2000 Manual on Uniform Traffic Control Devices (MUTCD), entitled "Control of Traffic Through Traffic Incident Management Areas," defines an incident as follows:

— A traffic incident is an emergency road user occurrence, a natural disaster, or a special event that affects or impedes the normal flow of traffic.

— The proposed MUTCD amendment classifies traffic incident severity by duration of incident. Incident classification levels include:

  a) Major: expected duration of more than 2 hours;

  b) Intermediate: expected duration of 30 minutes to 2 hours; and

  c) Minor: expected duration under 30 minutes.

— Planned special events having a duration of two hours fall within the classification of "major incident."

The Colorado Department of Transportation (DOT)—Region 6 maintains the following criteria for classifying a planned special event as a Level III Modified Incident, the highest Region 6 traffic incident severity level: special or planned events that have major impacts.

It is important to recognise that the impact of a planned special event on traffic and transit operations depends on a combination of several dynamic factors. Collectively, planned special event impact factors differ from those considered in determining the severity of other types of planned and unplanned events. As illustrated in Figure 2, the three core factors include travel demand, road/site capacity, and event operation.

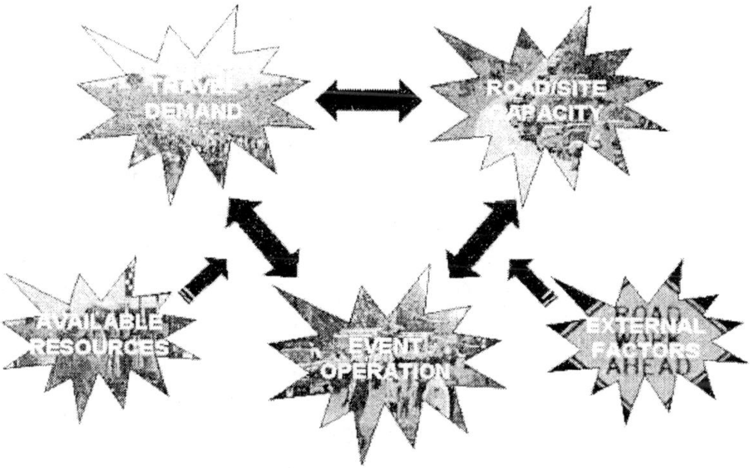

Figure 2. Planned Special Event Impact Factors

Available resources and external factors represent secondary aspects that also affect the impact a planned special event has on transportation system operations. Key considerations include.

— Travel demand refers to the expected number of event patrons and their arrival and departure rates. Modal split has a significant influence on the level of event impact, particularly on traffic operations. Event patrons may travel to the event via personal vehicle, transit, walking, or a combination of modes. A planned special event travel forecast involves estimating travel demand magnitude, travel demand rate, and modal split.

— Road/site capacity concerns the available venue access and parking background capacity in addition to the capacity of roadways and transit serving the event venue. Capacity must take into account: (1) background parking occupancy in parking areas serving the event venue and (2) volume of background traffic that normally traverses the road system serving the event venue. Capacity influences travel demand to a limited extent, as "seasoned" event patrons in some locales may choose to use transit to access an event venue, because of severe traffic congestion experienced in the past, although they may not represent regular transit users.

— Event operation essentially defines the scope of travel demand, including market area, and may reduce available background capacity because of event staging requirements. Event operations impact the effect a planned special event has on travel. For instance:

a) A venue may open earlier to better spread the rate of arrivals for a concert or sporting game.

b) Event patrons may be given special advance instruction on specific parking options.

c) An event organiser may relocate an event to a different venue when roadway capacity deficiencies can not be adequately mitigated.

d) On the other extreme, corporate hospitality tents at the 2003 Super Bowl in San Diego reduced the amount of available on-site parking from 19,600 spaces to 3,400 spaces.

— Available resources refer to the quantity of personnel and equipment available to plan for and conduct day-of-event travel management operations. The occurrence of regional/multi-venue events or other unplanned events may strain available stakeholder resources needed to manage a particular planned special event.

— External factors include concurrent roadway construction activities on roadway corridors serving a venue and prevailing weather conditions on the day-of-event. Weather conditions have a significant impact on attendance (e.g., travel demand) or the rate of arrivals and departures at some events. For example:

  a) Event patrons will attend an open-air sporting event in extremely hot weather, but patrons may bypass arriving at the venue early to tailgate, thus concentrating patron arrivals.

  b) Rain events may flood unpaved parking lots and venue access roads, rendering them impassable and reducing available road/site capacity. Rain events may also cause sharp arrival and departure rates in addition to safety problems.

When determining the level of impact each of the five stated planned special event factors has on travel, consider each of the following components:

— Duration: temporal impact.

— Extent: spatial impact or scope of area affected.

— Intensity: volume of impact.

Classification of Impacts

Jurisdictions have established defined planned special event impact classification levels for the purpose of determining:

— event permit requirements,

— transportation management plan deployment, and

— scope of potential impact on the transportation system.

Event Permit Requirements

A number of communities with planned special event permit guidelines have also developed criteria to categorise various sizes of planned special events. As a result, one proposed special event may have to meet more stringent permitting requirements than other events based on its severity classification. Decision criteria include expected attendance and scope of street closure.

Transportation Management Plan Deployment

Stakeholders often develop transportation management plans specific to a permanent venue, such as a stadium, arena, or amphitheater. Development of site access and parking plans usually occur during venue construction. Transportation agencies and law enforcement may develop traffic control plans, based on a generic or recurring event, for managing transportation operations on streets adjacent to the venue and/or corridors serving the venue during future planned special events. These programme planning activities do not focus on a single, known planned special event.

Therefore, stakeholders must establish transportation management plan deployment thresholds to ensure availability and placement of adequate resources to maintain satisfactory site and transportation operations during any future planned special event occurring at the venue. The parking and transportation management plan for Investco Field in Denver contains separate traffic management and operations plans, categorised under four attendance scenarios, for future planned special events occurring at the venue:

— Sold-out Denver Broncos (football) games.

— Other large events with an attendance of more than 60,000.

— Medium events with an attendance between 40,000 and 59,000.

— Small events with an attendance between 20,000 and 39,000.

The traffic management and operations plans for each scenario vary based on:

— event patron modal split prediction,

— site parking lot usage,

— Investco Field transit service, and

— level of personnel and equipment resources for traffic control in the vicinity of Investco Field.

Impact on the Transportation System

The State of Wisconsin and the City of Los Angeles assign event impact levels for a proposed planned special event:

The organisation of the Traffic Incident Management Enhancement (TIME) programme in southeastern Wisconsin includes a 40-plus agency Freeway Incident Management Team responsible for providing technical guidance toward TIME implementation. This group maintains a subcommittee on special events. The special events subcommittee proposed a concept of creating a special event traffic management planning tool applicable to any planned special event proposed in the greater Milwaukee metropolitan area.

The tool proves particularly useful for assessing the required multi-agency response to a planned special event proposed with relatively brief advance notice. Based on the input of information related to the previously described five event impact factors, the tool assigns one of five event impact levels to a proposed event. The following numerical thresholds define the five event impact levels:

— Traffic Condition Level 1 = 15

— Traffic Condition Level 2 = 25

— Traffic Condition Level 3 = 35

— Traffic Condition Level 4 = 45

— Traffic Condition Level 5 = 65

TIME stakeholders plan to develop an action plan corresponding to each identified planned special event level. The action plan will list recommended practices for stakeholders that regularly manage traffic during the occurrence of a planned special event, including the Wisconsin DOT—District 2, county highway departments, law enforcement, and event venue personnel. These recommended practices would detail required staffing levels, on-call equipment, alternate route usage, traffic signal system modifications, available transit options, and other information.

The City of Los Angeles DOT (LADOT) and Los Angeles Police Department (LAPD) maintain a database of planned special events scheduled to occur within the agencies' jurisdiction. The LADOT and LAPD assign an event impact level to each event to describe the general scope of each agency's involvement in advance planning and day-of-event traffic management. The event impact levels include:

— Level 1: Install and enforce temporary parking restrictions.

— Level 2: Level 1 and deployment of traffic officers (LAPD).

— Level 3: Level 2 and engineering/ATSAC support (LADOT).

— Level 4: Coordinated major event response effort.

ATSAC refers to LADOT's Automated Traffic Surveillance and Control System. Initially deployed for the 1984

Summer Olympic Games, ATSAC is a computer traffic signal system that monitors traffic conditions and system performance, selects appropriate traffic signal timing strategies, and performs equipment diagnostics and alert functions. Operators at the ATSAC Operations Center receive real-time information from signalised intersection detectors and signal controllers, and operators have access to closed-circuit television images at critical locations throughout the City.

Transportation system performance during a planned special event affects numerous stakeholders. Achieving seamless and efficient transportation operations between freeways, streets, parking facilities, and transit serving a special event venue requires a sound multidisciplinary, inter-jurisdictional, and inter-modal approach. The organisation and coordination of planned special event stakeholders is paramount to meeting the goals of planned special event management: achieving predictability, ensuring safety, and maximising efficiency.

Steps toward meeting this objective begin in the advance planning of traffic management plans and other initiatives and continues through implementation and day-of-event travel management. Planned special events can involve a wide range of stakeholders with diverse goals and incentives. One of the biggest challenges to consistently achieving effective planned special event management is coordinating and integrating the responses of all involved stakeholders, each with responsibility to serve the public, but with sometimes divergent priorities and performance objectives. Each stakeholder has its own norms, guidelines, sense of authority, and internal culture.

The involvement of multiple stakeholders can threaten the sense of security and authority of each, causing such groups to unconsciously deemphasise the public good each has set out to serve. As a result, the objectives of the collective stakeholder group are left unfulfilled. Several stakeholders active in the advance planning and management of planned special events also team to mitigate the occurrence of unplanned events, such as traffic incidents and other emergencies, through proactive planning and response.

These stakeholders include transportation agencies, law enforcement, and emergency service agencies. It should be recognised that the roles and responsibilities of stakeholders involved in managing unplanned events change under planned special events. However, the important partnerships and level of trust established between stakeholders carry over to groups formed to plan and manage planned special events. Figure 3 shows that advance planning and day-of-event management of travel for planned special events involves stakeholders comprising the following three distinct groups:

— The oversight team involves stakeholders participating in programme planning activities to improve the management of travel during future planned special events. These stakeholders include mid-to-upper level representatives of transportation agencies and law enforcement. Additional stakeholders include elected officials, regional organisations, and other government agencies. Members of an oversight team work to establish policies, regulations, procedures, and task forces for future application to a specific planned special event. Team members may interact with an event planning team, consulting on feasibility study results and evaluating conceptual transportation management plan components. Stakeholders may also work independent of the team to evaluate potential new technology applications that may improve their performance and capabilities while meeting team objectives.

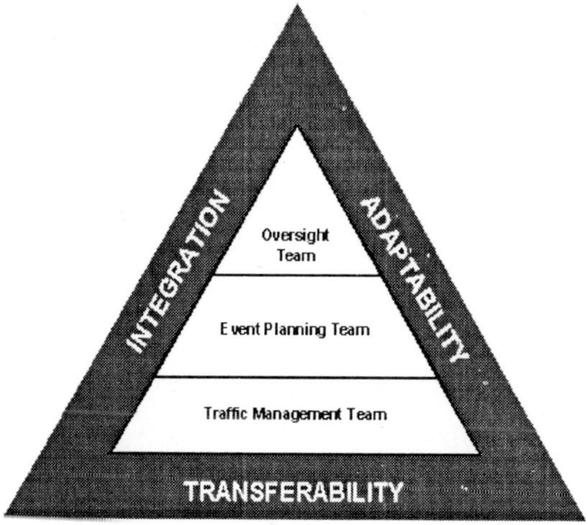

Figure 3. Planned Special Event Stakeholder Groups

— The event planning team involves stakeholders participating in event-specific operations planning and traffic management plan implementation tasks. Stakeholders comprising the oversight team typically have mid-level representatives serving on the event planning team. Other stakeholders include the event organiser, media, emergency service agencies, private industry, and the public. Due to the wide range of advance planning tasks and potential event management initiatives, an event planning team may create a number of satellite task forces. Example task forces include a communications subcommittee or task force on evaluating potential travel demand management strategies.

— The traffic management team involves stakeholders responsible for managing travel on the day-of-event. These stakeholders include operations managers and field personnel representing transportation agencies, law enforcement, the event organiser, media, and private industry. An event traffic management team typically interacts with the event planning team during implementation activities. The traffic management team may also debrief the oversight team and event planning team during post-event evaluation activities.

Major annual event or venue task forces exist in some jurisdictions that serve the role of both an oversight team and event planning team. The task force may meet year-round to mitigate lessons learned from past events, then expand to include additional event operations stakeholders as the next event nears. The success of each identified stakeholder group in meeting the goals of managing travel for planned special events depends on three criteria: integration, adaptability, and transferability:

— Integration refers to achieving stakeholder cooperation and coordination across disciplines and jurisdictional boundaries. Interagency resource sharing represents a product of such stakeholder coordination.

— Adaptability concerns the ability of stakeholders to adapt to new roles and responsibilities unique to managing travel for planned special events. These new roles may involve changes in stakeholder authority compared to roles under other types of planned and unplanned events.

— Transferability refers to maintaining continuous interagency communication, sharing of expertise to effect interagency training, and exchanging observations and lessons learned relative to stakeholder experiences.

The discussed criteria facilitates good management that, in turn, helps meet the needs of all road users and achieve satisfactory outcomes for each involved stakeholder.

2

Pre-event Research

The better research you conduct prior to the event, the more likely you are to produce an event that matches the planned outcomes of the organisers or stakeholders. For many years, public relations professionals and other marketing experts have realised the value of using research to pinpoint the needs, wants, desires, and expectations of prospective customers. Government leaders regularly conduct feasibility studies prior to authorising capital investments. These feasibility studies include exhaustive research.

An event is a product that is placed before the public with the reasonable expectation that they will attend. Therefore, it is imperative that you conduct careful and accurate consumer research to reduce the risk of nonattendance. The three types of research that are used for pre-event research are quantitative, qualitative, or a combination or hybrid of both. Matching the research type to the event is important and is determined by the goals of the research, the time allowed for conducting the research, and the funds available.

Techniques for Market Research

Before bringing a new product or service to market, the

inventor or manufacturer will conduct market research to determine the needs, wants, desires, and expectations of the target market. Whether your event is a new or a preexisting product, market research is required to determine how to obtain the very best position in a sometimes crowded marketplace. Typically, qualitative and, in most cases, focus group research is used for this purpose.

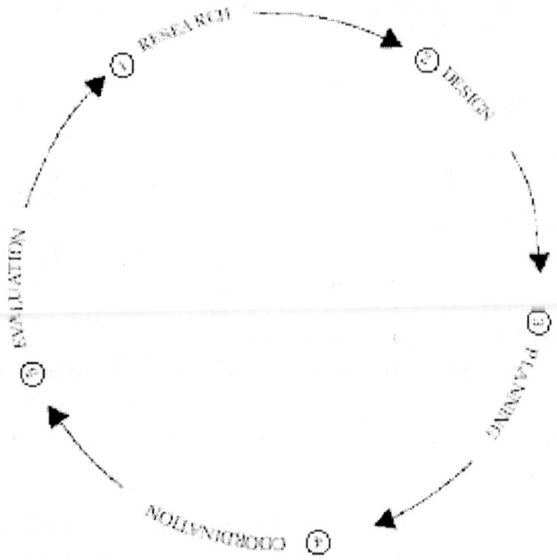

Figure 1. Event Management Process

Market research will help you determine the target or primary market as well as the secondary and tertiary markets for your event. Market research will also enable you to study the service levels expected by guests as well as the perceptions by internal stakeholders of the services currently being delivered. By studying the market in depth, you are able to spot emerging trends, develop new service delivery systems, and solve minor problems before they become major catastrophes.

Quantitative Research

Event Leaders primarily use quantitative research to determine demographic information such as gender, age, income, and other pertinent facts about the future market for an event. This research is relatively inexpensive to conduct and easy to tabulate and analyse with computers. Whether you use a written survey, in-person interview, or telephone interview method of construction, the research survey is of prime importance. To achieve the greatest possible response, offer a reward such as "enclose your business card and we will share the research findings with you," or offer an immediate incentive such as enclosing a $1 bill.

Qualitative Research

Market research consultants rely on qualitative research to probe for hidden meanings in quantitative studies. Qualitative research tells the research organisation what is beneath the numbers in quantitative research and, therefore, is an important step in the research process. This type of research may take the form of a focus group, participant/observer research, or a case study. Selecting the proper methodology depends on your goals, the time available, and the funding. The focus group is typically comprised of 8 to 12 people of similar background and experience who assemble for the purpose of discussion.

A trained facilitator leads the group through specific questions that will provide clues to the goals or outcomes desired from the research. A focus group may be one hour in length, although, in most cases, they last between 90 minutes and two hours. In some instances, a room with a one-way mirror is used to allow the other stakeholders to observe participants for subtle changes in body language, facial reactions, and other gestures that may reveal information in addition to their verbal opinion.

The focus group is audiotaped and the tapes are later transcribed and analysed to identify areas of agreement or discord. The participant/observer style of qualitative research involves placing the researcher in a host community to participate in and observe the culture of those being studied. For example, if you desire to determine whether or not a certain destination is appropriate for relocation of an event, you may wish to visit, participate, and observe for an extended period of time before making a decision. Interviews with key informants are essential to this research.

Qualitative research is generally more expensive than quantitative research due to the time that is involved in probing for deeper, more meaningful answers than only digits. The cost of training interviewers, the interviewer's time, the time for analysing the data, and other costs contribute to this investment. Although the cost is greater, many Event Managers require both qualitative and quantitative studies to validate their assumptions or research their markets.

Combined Research

In most cases, Event Managers use a combination of quantitative and qualitative research to make decisions about future events. This combined research allows the Event Manager to obtain large volumes of information in a costefficient manner using the quantitative method and then probe for hidden meanings and subtle feelings using the qualitative approach. Effective quantitative research has elements of qualitative research included to increase the validity of the questions.

Event Managers should use a small focus group or team of experts to review the questions before conducting a survey. These experts can confirm that a question is understandable and valid for the research being conducted.

Table 1 provides a simple way for Event Managers to determine what research methodology is most effective for their purpose.

Table 1. Selecting the Appropriate Pre-Event Research Method

Goal	Method
Collect gender, age, and income data	Written survey
Collect attitudes and opinions	Focus group
Examine culture of community	Participant/observer
Identify comparable characteristics	Case study
Collect demographic and psychographic data	Combined methods

The goals and required outcomes of the research, combined with the time frame and funding available, will ultimately determine the best method for your pre-event research. Regardless of the type of research you conduct, it is important that you take care to produce valid and reliable information.

Validity and Reliability

All research must be defended. Your stakeholders will ask you bluntly, "How do you know that you know?" If your research has high validity and reliability, you can provide greater assurance that your work is truthful Validity primarily confirms that your research measures what it purports to measure. For example, if you are trying to determine if senior citizens will attend an event, you must include senior citizens in your sample of respondents to ensure validity. Furthermore, the questions you pose to these seniors must be understandable to them to ensure that their responses are truthful and accurate.

Reliability helps prove that your research will remain truthful and accurate over time. Designing a collection instrument that has high validity and reliability is a challenging and timeconsuming task. You may wish to contact a university or college marketing, psychology, or sociology department for assistance by an experienced researcher in developing your instrument. Often, a senior-level undergraduate student or a graduate student may be assigned to help you develop the instrument and collect and analyse the data for college credit. The participation of the university or college will add credibility to your findings. Software applications such as Microsoft Excel should be used for analysing data.

Designing and collecting pre-event research is only the beginning of this important phase. Once you have analysed the data carefully and identified the implications of your research, as well as provided some recommendations based on your study, you must present the information to your stakeholders. The way that you do this will determine the level of influence you wield with stakeholders.

If the stakeholders are academics or others who have a research background, using tables or a written narrative may suffice. However, if, as is most often the case, stakeholders are unsophisticated with regard to research, you may instead wish to use graphs, charts, and other visual tools to illustrate your findings. To present your pre-event research findings effectively:

1. Determine your audience and customise your presentation to their personal communication learning style.
2. Describe the purpose and importance of the research.
3. Explain how the research was collected and describe any limitations.
4. Reveal your findings and emphasise the key points.
5. Invite questions.

Distributing a well-produced written narrative with copies of the information you are presenting will be helpful to the stakeholders, as they will require more time for independent study before posing intelligent questions. In the written narrative, include a section describing the steps you have taken to produce research that demonstrates high validity and reliability and list any independent organisations (such as a university or college) that reviewed your study prior to completion. Communicating your research findings is an essential phase in the research process. Prepare, rehearse, and then reveal your data thoughtfully and confidently. Summarise your presentation by demonstrating how the findings support the goals and objectives of your research plan.

How to Produce Effective Events

Following the economically rocky early 1990s, corporations, associations, governments, and other organisations began to analyse carefully why a meeting or event should occur. This solid reasoning should be applied to every event decision.

The first step is to ask: "Why must we hold this event?" There must be not one but a series of compelling reasons that confirm the importance and viability of holding the event.

The second step is to ask: "Who will the stakeholders be for this event?" Stakeholders are both internal and external parties. Internal stakeholders may be the board of directors, committee members, staff, elected leaders, guests, or others. External stakeholders may be the media, politicians, bureaucrats, or others who will be investing in the event. Conducting solid research will help you determine the level of commitment of each of these parties and better help you define who this event is being produced for.

The third step is to ask: "When will the event be held?" You must ask yourself if the research-through-evaluation time frame is appropriate for the size of this event. If this time period is not appropriate, you may need to rethink your plans and either shift the dates or streamline your operations. When may also determine where the event may be held.

The fourth step involves asking where the event will be held. Once you have selected a site, your work becomes either easier or more challenging. Therefore, this decision must be made as early as possible, as it affects many other decisions.

The fifth and final "W" is to determine from the information gleaned thus far what the event product is that you are developing and presenting. Matching the event product to the needs, wants, desires, and expectations of your guests while satisfying the internal requirements of your organisation is no simple task. What must be analysed carefully and critically to make certain that the why, who, when, and where are synergised in this answer. Once these five questions have been answered thoroughly, it is necessary to turn your deliberations to how the organisation will allocate scarce resources to produce maximum benefit for the stakeholders. SWOT (strengths, weaknesses, opportunities, threats) analysis provides a comprehensive tool for ensuring that you review each step systematically.

SWOT Analysis

Before you begin planning an event, SWOT (strengths, weaknesses, opportunities, threats) analysis usually must be implemented to underpin your decision-making. SWOT analysis assists you in identifying the internal and external variables that may prevent the event from achieving maximum success.

The strengths and weaknesses of an event are primarily considerations that can be spotted before the event actually takes place. Typical strengths and weaknesses of many events are shown in Table 2.

Table 2. Event Strengths and Weaknesses

Strengths	Weaknesses
Strong funding	Weak funding
Good potential for sponsors	No potential for sponsors
Well-trained staff	Poorly trained staff
Many volunteers	Few volunteers
Good media relations	Poor media relations
Excellent site	Weak site

The strengths and weaknesses may be uncovered through a focus group or through individual interviews with the major stakeholders. If the weaknesses outnumber the strengths and there is no reasonable way to eliminate the weaknesses and increase the strengths within the event planning period, you may wish to postpone or cancel the event.

Threats and Opportunities

Threats and opportunities are two key factors that generally present themselves either during an event or after it has occurred. However, during the research process, they should be considered seriously, as they may spell potential disaster for the event. Opportunities are activities that may be of benefit to an event without significant investment by your organisation. One example is that of selecting a year in which to hold an event that coincides with your community's or industry's 100th anniversary.

Your event may benefit from additional funding, publicity, and other important resources simply by aligning yourself with this hallmark event. Other possible beneficial outcomes, sometimes indirect, such as the potential of contributing to the event host's political image, are considered opportunities. Threats are activities that prevent you from maximising the potential of an event. The most obvious threat is weather; however, political threats may be just as devastating.

Local political leaders must buy into your civic event to ensure cooperation with all agencies. Political infighting may quickly destroy your planning. A modern threat is that of terrorism. The threat of violence erupting at an event may keep people from attending. A celebrity cancelling or not attending can also create a significant threat to the success of an event. Typical opportunities and threats for an event are listed in Table 3. You will note that, although strengths and weakness are often related, opportunities and threats need not be. Once again, in making a decision to proceed with event planning, your goal is to identify more opportunities than threats.

Table 3. Event Opportunities and Threats

Opportunities	Threats
Civic anniversary	Hurricanes and tornadoes
Chamber of Commerce promotion	Political infighting
Celebrity appearance	Violence from terrorism
Align with environmental cause	Alcoholic consumption
Tie-in with media	Site in bad neighborhood
Winning elections	Celebrity canceling or not attending
Devoloping more loyal employees	

All threats should be considered carefully and experts should be consulted to determine ways in which threats may be contained, reduced, or eliminated. SWOT analysis is a major strategic planning tool during the research phase. By using SWOT analysis, an Event Manager can not only scan the internal and external event environment but also can proceed to the next step, which involves analyses of the weaknesses and threats, and provide solutions to improve the event planning process. The research phase of the event administration process is perhaps most critical.

During this period you will determine through empirical research whether you have both the internal and external resources essential to make a decision to produce an effective event. Your ability to select the appropriate research methodology, design the instrument, and collect, analyse, interpret, and present the data will ultimately determine whether or not an event has sufficient strength for future success. The first pillar of the Event Management process-research-rests squarely in the centre of the other four supporting columns. Although each is equal in importance, the future success of an event depends on how well you conduct the research phase.

3

Designing of Events

Having researched your event thoroughly and determined that it is feasible, time may now be allotted to use the right side of the brain-the creative capacity to create a general blueprint for your ideas. There are numerous ways to begin this process, but it is important to remember that the very best event designers are constantly visiting the library, attending movies and plays, visiting art galleries, and reviewing periodicals to maintain their inspiration. This continuous research for new ideas will further strengthen the activities you propose for an event.

Mind Mapping and Brainstorming

Too often in volunteer-driven organisations, the very best ideas are never allowed to surface. This occurs because well-meaning volunteers (and some not so well-meaning volunteers) tell their colleagues that "this will never work" or "this is impossible at this time." Although their opinions are certainly valid, the process of shooting down ideas before they are allowed to be fully developed is a tragic occurrence in many organisations. Creativity must be encouraged and supported by Event Managers because, ultimately, the product you will offer is a creative art.

Creativity is an essential ingredient in every event management process. Therefore, when beginning the design phase of this Event Management process, conduct a meeting where creative people are encouraged to brainstorm the various elements of the event. The Event Manager is the facilitator of this meeting, and, in addition to various creative stakeholders, you may choose to invite other creative people from the worlds of theatre, dance, music, art, literature, and other fields.

Mind mapping allows an Event Manager to begin to pull together the random ideas and establish linkages that will later lead to logical decision making. Mind mapping is an effective way to synthesise the various ideas suggested by group members and begin to construct an event philosophy. The event philosophy will determine the financial, cultural, social, and other important aspects of the event. For example, if the sponsoring organisation is a not-for-profit group, the financial philosophy will not support charging high fees to produce a disproportionate amount of funds, or the tax status may be challenged.

Mind mapping allows you to sift through the ideas carefully and show how they support the goals of the event. By your doing this, an event philosophy begins to emerge. Those ideas that do not have a strong linkage or support the philosophy should be placed on a separate sheet of flipchart paper for future use.

Creativity in Event Managements

Special events require people with the ability to move easily between the left and right quadrants of the cerebellum. The right side of the brain is responsible for creative, spontaneous thinking, while the left side of the brain handles the more logical aspects of our lives. Event Managers must be both right- and left-brained to be able to function effectively. Therefore, if you have determined that one side of your brain is less strong than the other, you must take steps to correct this to achieve maximum success in Event Management.

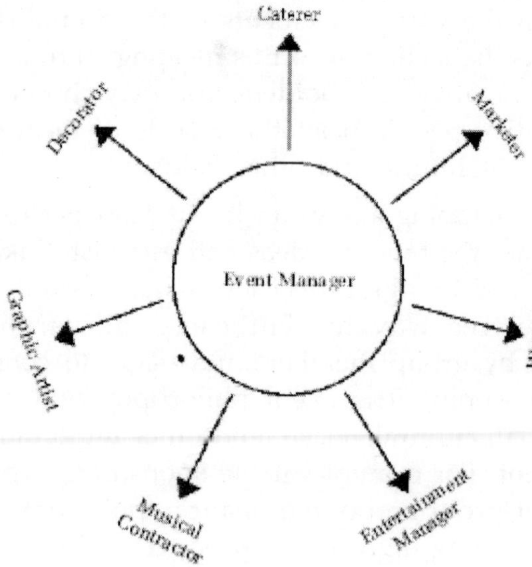

Figure 1. Creative Influences

Remember that developing creativity is a continuous process. The reason that some corporations put their advertising accounts out for review to other agencies periodically is to be sure that the current agency is working at its highest possible creative level. As an Event Manager, you too must strive for constant review of your creative powers to make certain that you are in high gear. Following are some tips for continuously developing your creativity:

1. Visit one art gallery each month.
2. Attend a live performance of opera, theatre, or dance each month.
3. Read great works of literature, on a continuing basis.

4. Enroll in a music, dance, literature, visual arts, or acting class or discussion group.
5. Apply what you are discovering in each of these fields to Event Management.

Perhaps the best way to stretch your creativity continually is to surround yourself with highly creative people. Whether you are in a position to hire creativity or must seek creative types through groups outside the office, you must find the innovators in order to practice innovation.

Needs Assessment and Analysis

Once you have completed the brainstorming and mind-mapping activities satisfactorily, it is time to make certain that your creative ideas perfectly match the goals and objectives of your event. This is accomplished through needs assessment and analysis.

Needs assessment and analysis enables you to create an event that closely satisfies the needs of your stakeholders. You actually began this process by asking "Why?" and "Who?" Now it is time to take it one giant step forward and survey the stakeholders to determine if your creative solutions will satisfy their needs.

To accomplish this part of the design phase, develop your ideas into a series of questions, query the key constituents for the event, and determine if the various elements you have created-from advertising to décor, from catering to entertainment, and everything in between-meet their expectations.

Once you are confident that you have assessed the needs of the stakeholders adequately and confirmed that you have, through analysis, determined how to satiate these needs, you are well prepared to confirm the final feasibility of your event design.

Feasibility

Feasibility simply means that you have looked at the event design objectively to determine if what you propose is feasible given the resources available. This is the final checkpoint before actual planning begins and, therefore, must be given adequate time for review.

Municipalities often engage professional engineers or other consultants to conduct lengthy feasibility studies before approving new construction or other capital expenditures. Although you may not need a battery of consultants, it is important for you to review all previous steps thoroughly when determining the feasibility of an event plan.

The three basic resources that will be required are financial, human, and political. Each of these resources may have varying degrees of importance, depending on the nature of the event. For example, a for-profit or large hallmark event will require significant financial investment to succeed. On the other hand, a not-for-profit event will rely on an army of volunteers, and, therefore, the human element is more important.

A civic event will require greater political resources to accomplish. Therefore, when assessing and analysing feasibility, first determine in what proportions resources will be required for the event. You may wish to weigh each resource to help prepare your analysis.

Financial considerations

You will want to know if sufficient financial resources are available to sustain development and implementation of the event. Furthermore, you must consider what will happen if the event loses money. How will creditors be paid? You will also want to know what resources you can count on for an immediate infusion of cash should the event require this to continue development. Finally, you must carefully analyse the cash-flow projections for the event to determine how much time is to be allowed between payables and receivables.

Human dimension

In assessing the feasibility of an event, you must not only know where your human resources will come from but how they will be rewarded (financially or through intangibles such as awards and recognition). Most important, you must know how they will work together as an efficient event team.

Political Issues

The increasingly important role of government leaders in event oversight must be viewed with a practiced eye. Politicians see events as both good (opportunities for publicity, constituent communications, and economic impact) and bad (drain on municipal services and potential for disaster).

When designing civic events, it is particularly important that you understand and enlist the support of politicians and their bureaucratic ministers to ensure smooth cooperation for your event. Furthermore, for all events, it is essential that you carefully research the permit process to determine if the event you have designed is feasible according to the code within the jurisdiction where the event will be held.

The research and design phases add to the event history once an event is approved. The approval process may be as simple as an acceptance by the client or as complex as requiring dozens of signatures from various city agencies that will interact with the event. Regardless of the simplicity or complexity of this step, you should view it as an important milestone that, once crossed, assures you that the plan has been reviewed and deemed reasonable and feasible, and has a high likelihood-to-succeed ratio.

All roads lead to official approval, whether in the form of a contract or as individual permits from each agency. Without official approval, an event remains a dream. The process for turning dreams into workable plans requires careful research, thoughtful design, and critical analysis. This could be called the "planning to plan phase," because it involves so many complex steps related to the next phase. However, once the approval is granted, you are on your way to the next important phase: the actual planning period.

4

PLANNING OF EVENTS

The planning period is typically the longest period of time in the event management process. Historically, this has been due to disorganisation. Disorganisation is best characterised by frequent changes resulting from substitutions, additions, or even deletions due to poor research and design. Ideally, the better the research and design, the simpler and briefer the planning period will be.

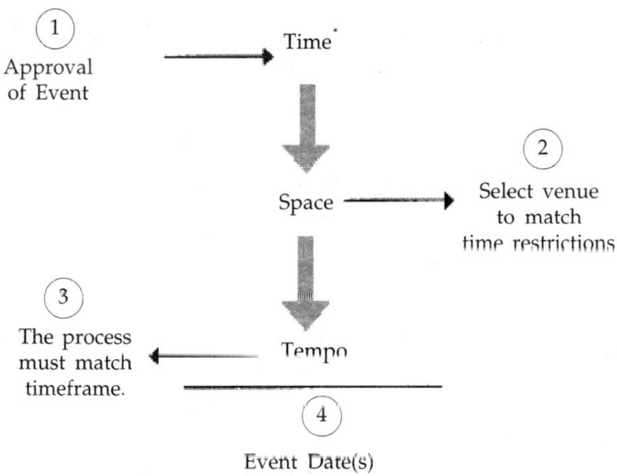

Figure 1. Time/Space/Tempo Laws

Since events are planned by human beings for other human beings, this theory is fraught with exceptions. However, your goal should be to develop a smooth planning process based on careful research and design procedures. The planning phase involves using the time/space/tempo laws to determine how best to use your immediate resources. These three basic laws will affect every decision you make; how well you make use of them will govern the final outcome of an event.

Time Management

The law of timing refers to how much time you have in which to act or react. The first question that many Event Managers ask the client is: When would you like to schedule the event? The answer to that question tells you how much time you have to prepare. Often, that timetable may seem incredibly short. The length of time available for planning and for actual production will dramatically affect the cost and sometimes the success of the event.

Budgeting your time is not an exact science but rather a dynamic experience that must be governed by the importance of each event. When budgeting your time for a proposed event, some independent Event Managers estimate the amount of time necessary for pre-event client meetings, site inspections, meetings with vendors, ongoing communications and contract preparations, actual event time from time of arrival through departure, and post-event billable time.

You can only estimate the time involved in these tasks and, therefore, must add a contingency time factor to each phase. By paying careful attention to the research and design phase, you will be able to budget your time more precisely. This is particularly true for the event itself. This part of planning involves when to arrive for a particular event, when to cue the appropriate musician or performer, when to take breaks, and of course, when to stop.

Planning the time of an event is as important as managing your planning time. The moment the client approves the date of an event, the Event Manager must begin assessing how the planning period will affect other business operations. Therefore, the law of timing sometimes requires that, when an un-reasonable time frame is allotted to produce an event professionally, the Event Manager must decline to accept the opportunity.

Space Management

The law of space refers to both the physical space where an event will be held and the time between critical decisions pertaining to the event. The relationship of timing to space is one that is constant throughout the entire event process. When selecting a venue for an event, the location and physical resources present will significantly affect the additional time that must be invested. If you select a historic mansion with elaborate permanent decor, less time will be required to decorate the site. By comparison, if you select a four-walled venue, such as a hotel or convention centre, significant time and expense must be invested to create a proper atmosphere for the event.

One of the primary considerations when selecting space is the age and type of guest who will be attending. Older guests may not be able to tolerate extreme temperatures, and this may preclude you from selecting an outdoor venue. For events with young children, you may or may not wish to select a site in a busy urban setting. Go back to the research and needs assessment phase, and review why this event is important and who the stakeholders are. Then select a venue specifically to match their needs, wants, and expectations.

The terms ingress and egress are important concepts when reviewing a potential venue. Ingress defines the entrances or access to the venue, and egress refers to the exits or evacuation routes. When considering ingress and egress, you must consider not only people, including those with disabilities, but also vehicles, props, possibly animals, and indeed any element that must enter or exit the site. Parking, public transportation, and other forms of transportation, including taxis, limousines, and tour buses, must also be considered when analysing a site. These considerations should include the number of parking spaces, including those for the disabled, the availability and security/safety of public transportation, and the time required to dispatch a taxi.

Tempo

The final law of event planning is concerned with the rate or tempo at which events take place during both production planning and the event itself. From the moment the client approves an agreement or authorises you to proceed with planning to the final meeting, you must be aware of the projected rate at which events will happen. Improved technology such as fax and online services has dramatically accelerated the process and the demands of clients to "do it now." However, "now" is often not as efficient as later.

When an Event Manager is pressured to deliver a product before it is fully developed, the results may be less than exemplary. Therefore, as you manage the rate at which tasks will be completed and events will occur, it is important to consider if each action is being performed at the best time. "Maybe" is not an acceptable response. To determine if this is the best moment for this task to be handled, ask yourself if you have sufficient information and resources to implement it. If not, try to delay the action until you are better prepared.

Establishing the proper tempo is not an exact science. Rather, like a conductor of an orchestra, you must allow your personal taste, energy, and experience to guide you as you speed up or slow down the tempo as required. Analysing the event site and estimating the time required for a project, the Event Manager is better able to set the tempo or schedule for the setup, production, and removal of the equipment. Without this advance analysis, the Event Manager becomes an orchestra conductor without benefit of a score, a musician without benefit of a maestro. Understanding the needs of guests also helps establish and adjust the tempo during an event.

If the guest is concerned primarily with networking, a leisurely time frame should be followed to allow for plenty of interaction. For example, while the transition from cocktails to dinner may be brisk when the programme is more important than networking, the transition may be slowed when the emphasis is on the connections the audience members make among themselves. Today, due to changing tastes, everyone is concerned with the food components and the final presentation.

These three basic laws, as old as human creation itself, govern the planning of all events. To become an expert Event Leader, you must master your ability to manage time in the most minute segments. You must develop the vision to perceive the strengths, weaknesses, opportunities, and threats of every space. Finally, you must be able to analyse the needs of your guests to set tempos that will ensure a memorable event.

Gap Analysis

Too often, Event Managers proceed by rote memory to produce an event in a style with which they are most familiar. In doing this, they often overlook critical gaps in the logical progression of event elements. Identifying these gaps and providing recommendations for closure is the primary purpose of gap analysis. This planning tool involves taking a long, hard look at event elements and identifying significant gaps in the planning that could weaken the overall progression of the plan.

The Event Manager has created a wide gap in his or her plan that must be closed to strengthen the overall event. Therefore, finding a secure indoor location in case of a weather emergency would be a good beginning toward closing this gap. Use a critical friend-a person whose expertise about the particular event is known to you-to review your plan and search for gaps in your logical thinking. Once you have identified the gaps, look for opportunities to close them. By implementing the findings from SWOT and gap analysis, you are able to begin executing your plan. This execution phase is known as coordination.

Coordination of Activities

Your ability to use your professional training and experience to make the correct decision will affect the outcome of the entire event. While it is true that Event Managers should maintain a positive attitude and see problems as challenges in search of the right solution, it is also important that you apply critical analysis to every challenge that comes your way. Following is a simple but effective way to make these decisions:

1. Collect all the information. Most problems have many sides to review.
2. Consider the pros and cons of your decision in terms of who will be affected.
3. Consider the financial implications of your decision.
4. Make a decision and do not look back.
5. Consider the moral and ethical implications of your decision.

Operations Planning

The event operations planning phase begins with stakeholders establishing a planning framework and schedule. The framework includes forming an event planning team, creating agreements, identifying performance goals and objectives, and deciding on mitigation assessment and approval protocol. Special considerations evolve from reviewing the event operations characteristics of a particular special event (e.g., risk assessment) in addition to past successes and lessons learned. These considerations weigh heavy on traffic management plan requirements, and stakeholders must address issues affecting community residents and businesses through public outreach efforts early in the planning phase in order to ensure proper mitigation and non-conflict with traffic management plan specifications.

Coordination and Role of Stakeholders

The event planning team handles tasks associated with event-specific operations planning and traffic management plan implementation. Table 1 lists the primary responsibilities of the event planning team under the event operations planning phase. The event planning team consists of a diverse group of stakeholders with either event operations or community interest as their primary concern. The success of the event planning team depends on achieving strong coordination among participating team stakeholders.

Table 1. Event Planning Team Responsibilities During the Event Operations Planning Phase

Responsibilities
• Perform feasibility study. • Develop traffic management plan. • Evaluate travel demand management initiatives.

Formation of Event Planning Team

An event planning team forms as a result of either: (1) coordination among traffic operations agencies, transit agencies, law enforcement agencies, and event organisers that represent the core event planning team stakeholders or (2) designation by a committee on special events within a regional transportation management organisation, such as a traffic incident management programme.

— The former typically describes event planning teams formed in response to local planned special events affecting few jurisdictions, such as events occurring in rural or urban areas.

— The latter may occur in metropolitan areas where planned special events happen frequently, thus warranting an on-call event planning team.

A regional transportation committee on special events features stakeholders that have achieved interagency coordination through past, cooperative travel management efforts.

— Stakeholder representatives have first-hand knowledge of the roles, resources, and capabilities of each committee participant.

— Stakeholders commonly include traffic operations agencies, law enforcement, transit agencies, event organisers or venue operators, and the media.

— Committees in metropolitan areas may create task forces for specific planned special event venues or recurring planned special events (e.g., annual fairs, fireworks displays, parades, etc.). The committee or task force generally meets and performs event operations planning tasks on an as-needed basis. The group may also convene regularly (e.g., weekly, monthly, or quarterly) to review programme planning efforts for future planned special events.

Prior to initiating the event operations planning process, the core event planning team should adopt a mission, or purpose, and solicit buy-in from public agency stakeholders, the community, and other event support stakeholders. In identifying pertinent jurisdictions, the event planning team may consider contacting stakeholders within a certain distance (e.g., five miles) of the event venue.

The event planning team can obtain buy-in from community interest stakeholders more easily when a core group of stakeholders already exists, including public agencies. Elected officials and the public can serve as advocates for the event planning team; therefore, participation from these stakeholders should occur early in the event operations planning phase.

In establishing an event planning team, the core stakeholders must develop a working trust with each other. This trust results when stakeholders realise that a planned special event necessitates the same relationships cultivated in daily traffic and incident management.

A joint operations policy or other memoranda of understanding strengthens the cooperative bond among core stakeholders. These agreements identify common goals and responsibilities of the partnering agencies. Consensus among stakeholders builds interagency coordination and an understanding of each agency's responsibility. Key elements to consider include:

— Participating stakeholders must recognise that the motivations of individual agencies may differ from the event planning team's concerns as a result of their day-to-day responsibilities.

— Although the event planning team does not have authority over individual stakeholders, the planning team must realise that possible conflicts may exist between the team's objectives and a stakeholder's primary responsibility. Understanding this is key to overcoming such a problem; yet, the team can foster a cooperative spirit among stakeholders by emphasising that participants own a part of the event planning team's common goals.

— Stakeholders must remain focused on the goals and objectives of the event planning team in order to effectively support and contribute in the event operations planning process. This includes concentrating on tasks that can be successfully accomplished collectively.

Common barriers to the event planning team's progress include resource constraints and jurisdictional barriers.

— Resource or funding constraints surface when stakeholders assign a lower priority to the planned special event. In satisfying individual and team goals, stakeholders may have to make temporary project and programme sacrifices, in terms of personnel and equipment reassignrnent, to provide adequate benefits to the event operations planning effort.

— Jurisdictional barriers arise when two or more stakeholders are unclear on their duties and responsibilities. Do not allow participating agencies to feel left out. At the time of buy-in, the event planning team must indicate which stakeholders are required on an as-needed basis. The team must have the ability to communicate effectively with stakeholders having a peripheral involvement in the overall planning effort.

Planning Risk Assessment

Based on the type and purpose of a planned special event, there exists potential scenarios where event patron or non-attendee behaviour may cause overcrowded conditions in the vicinity of an event venue and/or create unplanned road closures. The event planning team must assess the nature of a proposed event and determine the need to incorporate special contingency plans in response to potentially dangerous situations that will interfere with the planned travel management on the day-of-event.

Table 2 lists four notable event-oriented risk scenarios associated with some planned special events.

Table 2.Event-Oriented Risk Scenarios

Event-Oriented Risk		Example Scenario
Demonstration or protest	—	Any event that is political in nature or invokes social concern.
	—	Political conventions and parades
Ticketless event patrons causing overcrowding	—	Sold-out sports championship games
	—	Sold-out concerts involving select performers
Fan celebration	—	Response to city or school sports team winning a championship.
Event patron violence	—	Motorcycle rally violence between patrons and/or participants.

This section further describes these scenarios and highlights example case studies that illustrate resulting impacts on advance planning and/or day-of event operations.

Demonstration or Protest

Certain political or socially controversial planned special events may provoke a demonstration or protest. Those attending the demonstration represent non-attendees, and the event planning team often has little or no advance information regarding the demonstration's specific location and time of occurrence. The event planning team should obtain access to relevant law enforcement intelligence reports regarding potential demonstrations to develop an effective travel management contingency plan. The threat of an unplanned road closure should prompt the event planning team to consider developing an alternate route contingency plan detailing the personnel and equipment resources necessary to effect an immediate diversion of traffic.

Overcrowding

The occurrence of sports championship games or major concerts at venues having a defined sell-out capacity may attract ticketless event patrons not accounted for in event travel forecasts and impact mitigation strategies. After the event organiser unveiled a comprehensive security and traffic management plan that included using advance checkpoints to turn away any vehicle that contained a ticketless occupant, county executives overturned their decision and issued a permit.

Fan Celebration

Another severe impact risk associated with sports championship games involves fan celebrations that occur when a city sports team wins a championship at home. In this case, the traffic management team charged with managing travel during event egress must also mitigate traffic impacts caused by non-attendees converging on the venue site and unruly fans disrupting traffic and pedestrian flow.

Event Patron Violence

An outbreak of violence among event patrons warrants special security precautions to contain and capture potential suspects. Law enforcement may initiate a road closure as a first response to discourage people from entering and leaving the region where the violence took place.

TRAVEL PLANNING FOR SPECIAL EVENTS

The goals of managing travel for planned special events include achieving predictability, ensuring safety, and maximising efficiency. Table 3 states performance objectives, for the previously defined classes of transportation system users, applicable to satisfying the overall goal of operations efficiency and safety. In meeting these performance objectives, the event planning team must target the goal of achieving predictability during the event operations planning phase.

Table 3. Transportation System Operations Performance Objectives for Planned Special Events

User Class	Performance Objective
Event patron	- Minimise travel delay to/from the event. - Minimise conflicts between pedestrians and vehicles. - Minimise travel safety hazards. - Minimise impact of traffic incidents. - Disseminate accurate, timely, and consistent traveller information. - Increase automation of traffic control. - Maximise site access service flow rates.
Non-attendee road user	- Minimise travel delay on major thoroughfares, freeways and major arterials. - Minimise impact on commuter and trucker travel time reliability. - Maintain required parking and access for local residents and businesses. - Maintain unimpeded access for emergency vehicles
Transit user	- Maintain scheduled travel times. - Minimise transit bus dwell times. - Maintain required transit station parking for non-attendee transit users.

Table 4 presents common, easy-to-measure measures of effectiveness for assessing the performance objectives that describe traffic operations.

Table 4. Measures of Effectiveness for Assessing Performance Objectives

Location	Measure of Effectiveness
Venue parking areas	- Occupancy and turnover rate - Arrival and departure service rate - Time to clear parking lots
Intersections	- Vehicle delay - Queue length
Freeways and streets	- Travel time and delay - Traffic volume to capacity ratio - Traffic speed - Number and location of crashes and other incidents - Traffic incident clearance time

The event planning team should consider field studies to quantify existing MOEs at key roadways and intersections to calibrate capacity analysis software and computer simulation models applied during traffic management plan development. The identified MOEs represent day-of-event performance evaluation data, useful for: (1) making real-time adjustments to the traffic management plan on the day-of-event, (2) conducting a post-event evaluation of transportation system performance, and (3) referencing during advance planning for future event occurrences.

Event Planning Schedule and Deliverables

Two deliverables, produced by the event planning team during the event operations planning phase, include the feasibility study and the traffic management plan, designed to mitigate impacts identified in the feasibility study. Travel demand management represents a key component of the overall process when forecasted traffic demand levels approach or exceed available roadway capacity.

In Figure 2 illustrates a high-level event operations planning schedule for an event planning stakeholder group. The figure lists advance planning activities and potential stakeholder meetings and public hearings in a timeline relative to the planning deliverables. The schedule indicates other stakeholder planning initiatives, such as the development of a specialised transit plan to reduce event traffic demand.

The event planning team should:

— Obtain a completed special event permit application and commence work on the event feasibility study no later than 60 days prior to the event.

— Start developing the event traffic management plan and obtain all initial public input and recommendations no later than 30 days before the event.

— Set aside the final 14 days prior to the event for implementation activities in addition to event information dissemination.

The planning schedule provides a generic timeline, recognising that actual event operations planning schedules vary considerably. For instance, some major, roving planned special events, such as the U.S. Golf Open, require an event operations planning phase spanning more than one year.

Public Outreach

Planned special events that may impact adjacent neighbourhoods and businesses usually require public involvement to address related concerns. The public represents individual residents, businesses, and associated community groups.

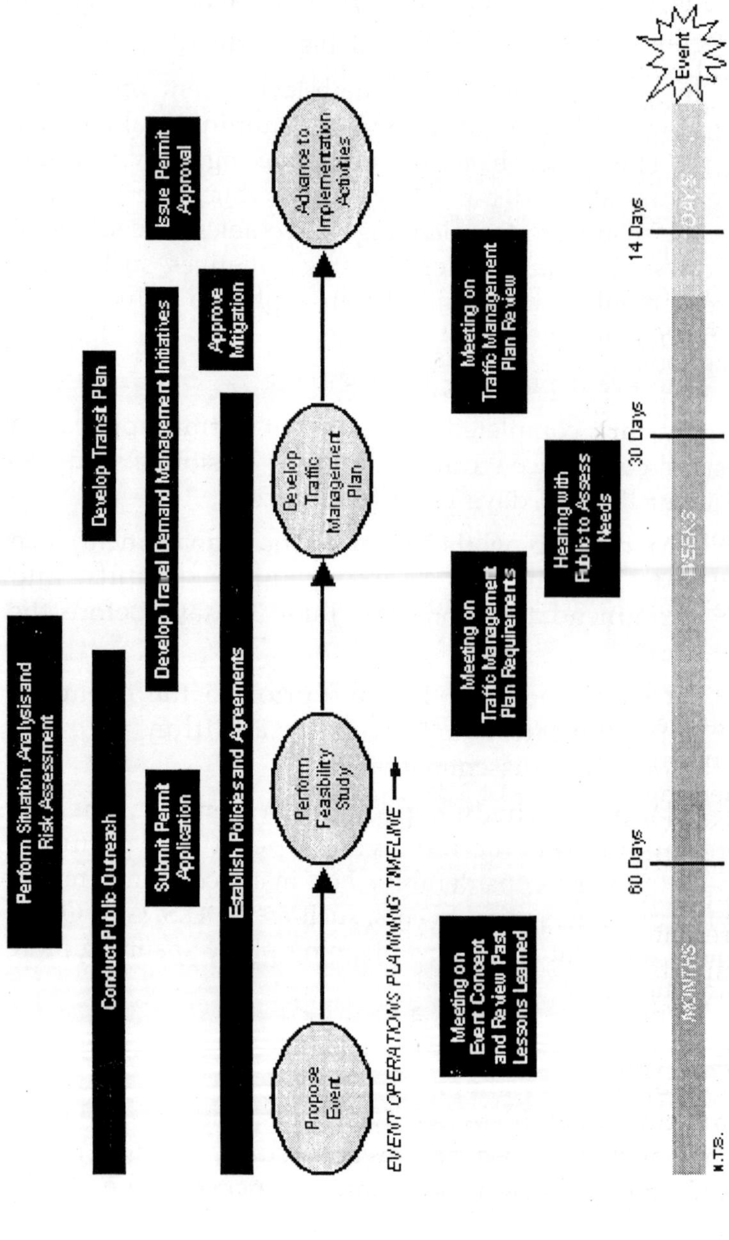

Figure 2. Event Operations Planning Schedule

Public outreach activities initiated early in the event operations planning phase can reveal important issues that local residents and businesses may have. Soliciting these concerns through public involvement, and addressing the issues in the planning process, can improve relations and day-of-event operations.

Street use events or other planned special events that take place at venues located adjacent to residential and/ or commercial districts may significantly impact non-attendee mobility and community quality of life. Specific neighbourhood impact issues include heavy traffic demand on local streets and event patron use of available local on-street parking. These issues arise because, in some instances, event patrons may find on-street parking in residential neighbourhoods and business districts affords more convenient ingress and egress. In addition, illegal parking fines may not exceed, or significantly exceed, the fee charged at designated venue parking areas.

Initiation of public outreach efforts includes stakeholders, such as a traffic operations agency or law enforcement, holding initial and regular meetings with community groups and local elected officials. At these meetings, the event planning team should present the scope of the event in enough detail to solicit quality input and buy-in from public stakeholders. Concerns revealed in this process should be addressed, and feasible solutions presented, so that the public stakeholders feel assured that impacts will be mitigated to their satisfaction.

The event planning team and public stakeholders should identify potential problems prior to the development of the traffic management plan. These problems can be identified by first understanding the event scope with consideration given to current neighborhood traffic and parking restrictions, traffic management plans deployed during past planned special events, and identified problems experienced during past events. With this information, the public stakeholders can make informed decisions and provide valuable input to the event planning team.

Stakeholder Review

Stakeholder review concentrates on the identification and proposed mitigation of event travel impacts. Effective and rapid stakeholder review of event operations planning products requires:

1) an annotated planning timeline,
2) a review process, and
3) performance standards.

Annotated Planning Timeline

In cases where an event planning team collectively develops a feasibility study, traffic management plan, and associated mitigation strategies, an annotated planning timeline proves effective for monitoring team progress. The agency maintained a responsibility matrix listing each action item, the stakeholder responsible, the due date, and the present deployment status. An event planning team should establish an annotated planning timeline early in the event operations planning phase and use the tool to guide subsequent team meeting agendas as stakeholders develop event impact mitigation strategies and tactics.

Review Process

Adopting a formal review process reduces unnecessary delay in producing event operations planning deliverables required to stage a planned special event. Key aspects to be considered include:

— The review process should feature the oversight team monitoring and reviewing plans developed by the event planning team.

- The oversight team typically consists of mid-to-upper level representatives of transportation agencies and law enforcement in addition to elected officials and ranking officials of other public agencies.
- A regional organisation may assume the duties of an oversight team.
- Under a formal review process, an event planning team may seek oversight team approval of a feasibility study scope or conceptual traffic management plan prior to commencing work on the final deliverable. Both stakeholder groups interact again to review feasibility study results and final traffic management operations plans.
- Some jurisdictions have a champion charged with resolving institutional and operations issues affecting travel management for planned special events. These champions have the position to mitigate issues hampering the event operations planning process. Therefore, they should administer the review process.
- Jurisdictions should have an alternate official ready to replace the current champion should that person resign from present duty.

Performance Standards

A review of various transportation system operations performance objectives and associated measures of effectiveness that stakeholders may use to monitor system performance on the day-of-event and, in turn, evaluate travel management efforts. During the event operations planning phase, stakeholders must set and agree to performance standards used to assess traffic impact mitigation proposals. These performance standards typically represent level of service (LOS) measures applicable to freeway and street segments, freeway junctions, and roadway intersections.

Stakeholders assigned to develop mitigation strategies or review planned special event impacts on traffic should reference jurisdiction Traffic Impact Study guidelines defining accepted LOS thresholds. The LOS thresholds likely vary by roadway classification. In urban and metropolitan areas, jurisdictions may deem an LOS D, describing high-density stable flow, acceptable for freeways, arterials, and major intersections.

Similarly, an LOS C, describing stable flow, may represent the allowable threshold for local streets and intersections. Small urban and rural areas may have more stringent requirements. Jurisdictions may relax their performance standards and allow LOS E operation, describing unstable capacity flow, on major roadway facilities for infrequent planned special events.

Special Policies and Agreements

The establishment of special policies and agreements to support planning and day-of-event management of planned special events facilitates efficient stakeholder collaboration and defines important event support stakeholder services that may be incorporated into a traffic management plan for a particular planned special event. These initiatives improve interagency relationships, clarify decision-making responsibilities and expectations, and secure on-call services and agency actions.

For instance, a particular policy or agreement may intuitively support a contingency response plan to mitigate unanticipated congestion delay on the day-of-event. Stakeholders may develop policies and agreements specific to a particular planned special event or for all planned special events in a region. Because of the potential significant time to develop and approve a particular policy or agreement, stakeholders should establish these initiatives early in the event operations planning phase or during the programme planning phase.

Table 5 summarises four types of policies and agreements involving stakeholders responsible for event operations planning and/or day-of-event operations.

Table 5. Summary of Policies and Agreements Applicable to Managing Planned Special Events

Item	Example Application
Interagency agreement	- Joint operations policy between stakeholders that establishes a shared role regarding event operations planning and day-of-event travel management. - Memorandum of understanding defining stakeholder roles and responsibilities. - Mutual-aid agreement facilitating resource sharing and/or reimbursement for services.
Standard street use programme event routes	- Routes established under the planning phase for recurring street use events such as parades and races.
Toll facility congestion policy	- Suspension of tolls during periods of heavy congestion.
Public-private towing agreement	- On-call towing and recovery services during a special event.

Interagency agreement

Interagency agreements include a joint operations policy, memorandum of understanding, or mutual-aid agreement between two or more stakeholders. Table 6 lists components of interagency agreements.

Table 6. Components of Interagency Agreements

Component
- Advance planning duties and responsibilities
- Day-of-event duties and responsibilities
- Organisation
- Resource sharing
- Funding reimbursement mechanisms

Stakeholders may also strike an interagency agreement, during the event operations planning phase, applicable to a specific planned special event.

Standard street use event routes

The development and use of standard street use event routes reduces the level and complexity of event operations planning tasks and overall planning time. In establishing such standard routes for parades and/or street races, stakeholders simplify planning tasks, thus creating a more efficient event operations planning process. The routes specify appropriate event starting and ending points coupled with staging areas for participant assembly and disbanding.

Use of a standard street use event route offers the following advantages:

- Allows reuse of traffic management and operations plans, with minor modifications as necessary.
- Realises a cost savings for stakeholders.
- Allows for the development of standard signs, specific to the event route and associated alternate routes for background traffic, that may be reused for future street use events.
- Allows event patrons and non-attendee road users to become familiar with traffic patterns during recurring street use events, thus minimising potential traffic problems on the day-of-event.

Toll facility congestion policy

Suspension of toll collections on turnpikes and other toll facilities during periods of heavy congestion represents a new policy concept aimed at reducing congestion and the occurrence of traffic incidents at toll plazas. A toll facility congestion policy represents a congestion mitigation strategy applicable to planned special events.

Public-private towing agreement

Private towing companies perform a specific functional activity in traffic incident management, that is, removal of disabled or wrecked vehicles, spilled cargo, and debris from an incident site. Law enforcement and traffic operations agencies alike have recognised the indispensable role private towing companies have in effecting incident removal and restoring the affected road section back to normal operation. Public agencies commonly enter into agreements with one or more commercial towing companies to secure on-call traffic incident clearance services, or at a minimum, the agencies maintain a contact list of local private towing companies. Traffic incident management represents a key consideration in event operations planning. Event planning team stakeholders may establish event-specific public-private towing agreements to secure on-site towing and recovery services.

Feasibility Study

The structure and approach of a planned special event feasibility study resembles a Traffic Impact Study required for planned developments, as illustrated in Figure 3. The figure shows the sequential steps in preparing a feasibility study for a planned special event.

The feasibility study gauges the impact a proposed event has on traffic and parking operations in the vicinity of the venue. It determines if a particular planned special event will cause travel problems, where and when the problems will occur, and the magnitude of each identified problem using various MOEs. Initially, the study is conducted without roadway capacity improvements or initiatives to reduce travel demand. Once the feasibility study identifies event travel problems, practitioners can take steps to mitigate transportation system deficiencies.

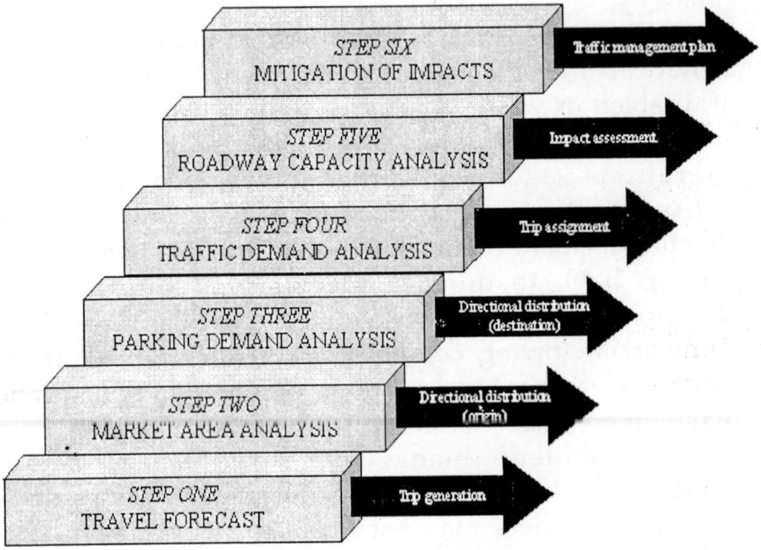

Figure 3. Feasibility Study Analysis Steps

These results define the scope of the traffic management plan required to successfully manage travel for a planned special event.

Input Data Requirements

Feasibility study input data requirements reflect measures of the three core factors that determine the impact of the event: travel demand, road/site capacity, and event operation. Travel demand data is used to develop the event travel forecast and to determine the event area of impact. Background traffic data describes the scope of available roadway and parking capacity for event patron traffic. Information regarding the venue area assists in identifying possible event patron trip origins. For example, a venue located in a downtown area may attract a significant number of patrons arriving from work, thus possibly reducing the number of transit or vehicular trips generated. Events having a regional or greater scope may involve a significant number of patrons staying at area hotels. To increase travel forecast accuracy and meet the goal of achieving predictability, practitioners should research appropriate historical data.

The identification and quantification of site and transportation system capacity involves performing a full inventory of the transportation system infrastructure serving the event venue. This includes obtaining data on roadway geometrics and associated regulations. An inventory of freeway facilities should include the capacity of such freeway components as ramp junctions and weaving sections. In addition, street traffic control devices and signal timing plans must be identified and saturation flow rates determined.

Event operation characteristics impact both travel demand and available capacity. The knowledge of certain event logistics, combined with available historical data, can help predict the rate of event patron arrivals and departures over time. Practitioners, in tandem with the event organiser, must also identify the scope of road closures and parking area needed just to stage the event.

Travel Forecast

Travel forecast analysis involves estimating:

1) modal split,

2) event traffic generation, and

3) traffic arrival rate.

Event planning team stakeholders that typically collaborate on this analysis include a traffic operations agency, traffic engineering consultant, transit agency, and event organiser.

The event organiser supplies key input data regarding event operation. The transit agency assists in estimating modal split. The traffic operations agency or traffic engineering consultant performs the analysis, and either stakeholder may research historical traffic and parking data or maintain a data archive related to operations for similar planned special events.

Modal split

Under the scope of a feasibility study, modal split concerns identifying the existing modes of travel event patrons will use to access the event venue site. Common travel modes include personal automobile, public transit, and walking. Public transit refers to scheduled bus transit or commuter rail. Transit agencies may assist in determining a base transit split, without service incentives or promotion, for patrons travelling to/from the event.

Commuter rail or other people mover systems exist in several metropolitan areas across the Nation and usually provide regular service to city stadium and arena venues. Transit availability includes scheduled express and charter bus service operating from other cities, suburban park and ride lots, and city neighbourhoods.

Travel time, travel convenience, parking accessibility and cost weighs significantly on an event patron's decision to drive or utilise an alternate mode of travel. This likely represents another contributor to the high transit split in the San Francisco example, where Pacific Bell Park resides adjacent to the downtown area. Other modes of travel include bicycle and taxi.

Walking trips deserve consideration in modal split estimates for planned special events occurring at downtown venues. Practitioners must consider the proximity of employment centres, residential developments, and hotels to a planned special event venue before dismissing walking as a viable travel mode. Venues located on university campuses typically draw a measurable percentage of walking trips. Surveys for college football games have reported as many as 10 to 25 percent of event patrons arriving by foot. Practitioners can best obtain measured data on planned special event modal split through conducting a survey of event patrons.

Event traffic generation

Unlike other traffic generators such as commercial developments, planned special event practitioners typically have advance knowledge of event attendance and, in turn, can develop traffic generation estimates via vehicle occupancy factors. On the other hand, traffic generation rates, based on event traffic volume or parking occupancy data, may not be appropriate for transfer and application from one special event to another. Too many variables exist with regard to event category, event logistics, event popularity, weather, and parking characteristics. Event operations and other external variables affect any application of historical data to future events.

Table 7 outlines a two-step process for forecasting event traffic generation. Input data includes a modal split estimate since the traffic generation forecast aims to estimate the number of event-generated trips by personal automobile. In the absence of a daily attendance estimate, practitioners can use percentage of venue capacity as a base. However, many continuous events or street use events do not have a pre-specified venue capacity. Continuous events, such as fairs and festivals, often run for two or more days. Attendance generally fluctuates greatly from day to day, with Saturday operations yielding the highest daily attendance.

A study of two day (Saturday/Sunday) festivals in West Virginia indicated 58 percent of the total festival attendance was on Saturday. The same study noted the following total event attendance distribution for three-day festivals: 20 percent on Friday, 50 percent on Saturday, and 30 percent on Sunday. It should be recognised that daily attendance reflects scheduled headline entertainment or other main festival events.

Table 7. Traffic Generation Forecast Process

Component	Detail
Input Data	• Daily attendance • Percent automobile trips • Vehicle occupancy factor
Method	***Step 1***. (Daily Attendance) x (Percent Automobile Trips) = Person Trips Via Automobile ***Step 2***. (Person Trips) / (Vehicle Occupancy Factor) = Vehicle Trips
Result	- Number of vehicle trips by personal automobile both to and from the event

Vehicle occupancy factors can serve as the basis for estimating event-generated traffic. A discrete/recurring event at a permanent venue that occurs on the weekend will likely have a higher vehicle occupancy factor due to families and groups of tailgaters. A vehicle occupancy factor of 2.5 persons per vehicle represents a common assumption, however for forecasting purposes, practitioners should consider a range of factors from 2.2 to 2.8 depending on local conditions.

In order to estimate peak traffic volumes generated by an event, practitioners must estimate the time and scope of peak traffic flow during event ingress and egress. Traffic arrival and departure rate indicates the peak period of event-generated traffic. The rate is used to determine the following key parameters for input into the traffic demand analysis:

(1) peak period time and

(2) percent of total event-generated traffic within the peak period.

Event operation characteristics that influence traffic arrival and departure rates include:

— Event time and duration—e.g., specific start time, abrupt end time, continuous operation.

— Event time of occurrence—e.g., day/night, weekday/weekend.

— Audience accommodation—e.g., reserved seating, general admission.

— Event type—e.g., sports/concert, fair/festival, parade/race.

The temporal share of event patron arrivals vary considerably by event type and requires prediction by practitioners. Traffic arriving to an event can potentially cause greater impacts to background traffic mobility than event departure traffic. This is attributed to arrival traffic typically travelling from high-capacity roadway facilities to low-capacity facilities. Roadway congestion that occurs during event ingress may create queue spillbacks to freeways and major streets, thus impacting background traffic.

Drivers departing an event venue site generally have little or no choice of exit routes. Roadway capacity constraints include freeway entrance ramps and turning movements to arterials and other major collector roadways. Departing traffic queues are usually constrained to the venue access roadway and spillback into the parking areas. Due to high traffic arrival concentration, practitioners may consider estimating a peak 15-minute traffic arrival rate and associated peak hour factor for roadway capacity analysis. With regard to continuous events, peak traffic arrival rate generally occurs immediately prior to the event start.

Since event patrons do not place a high priority on meeting a continuous event start time, the concentration of continuous event arrivals is relatively low compared to other event categories. The peak level of event-generated traffic demand may occur during the middle of a continuous event operating period when both event arrival and departure traffic traverse the roadway system as patrons come and go from the event.

Practitioners may use event patron travel surveys in addition to historical event-generated traffic volume and/or parking occupancy counts to estimate the traffic arrival rate and peak time of occurrence. It should be noted that weather conditions, particularly for continuous events and street use events, may significantly skew data. Thus, practitioners must exercise great care when developing future event estimates from historical data.

Market Area Analysis

A market area analysis identifies the origin and destination of trips to and from a planned special event. The analysis focuses on developing a regional directional distribution of event patron trips to/from an event site via personal automobile. The site refers to the collective parking areas serving the venue. A regional directional distribution specifies: (1) the freeway and arterial corridors serving the venue site and (2) the percent split and volume of event-generated automobile trips traversing each corridor. Table 8 summarises three analysis methods used to define a planned special event market area.

Table 8. Market Area Analysis Methods

Method	Description
Travel time analysis	- Determine population distribution within travel time threshold of event venue.
Distance analysis	- Determine population distribution within distance radius of event venue.
Origin location analysis	- Determine weighted distribution of known origins by place or zip code.

Travel time analysis

Practitioners can apply a travel time analysis or distance analysis to estimate the market area for any planned special event. Continuous events or street use events that do not offer advance ticket sales typically require a market analysis based on travel time or distance and referencing area population distribution.

Multiple travel time zones allow users to perform a weighted analysis of population distribution. Practitioners should categorise area population within each travel time zone by zip code or, for a 15 minute threshold or less, by census tract. Most geographic information systems and computer mapping tools generate spreadsheets identifying all spatial population categories within each travel time zone.

Using the spreadsheet, practitioners can assign a freeway or arterial corridor, serving the event venue site, to each defined population category. The population distribution among roadway system corridors constitutes the regional directional distribution for the planned special event. Practitioners can also incorporate Census socioeconomic data into an analysis as necessary.

The described travel time analysis methodology applies to a distance analysis as well. Instead of travel time thresholds, users define distance thresholds. Practitioners should exercise care in developing a planned special event market area by travel time or absolute distance to the event venue site:

— In the case of continuous events or street use events, the market area must incorporate only the community or region the event is staged for.

— Discrete/recurring events at a permanent venue, such as professional/major college sporting events or major concerts, warrant an expanded market area.

— A travel time or distance analysis for these events should not reflect a sensitivity to travel time or distance at the city/suburb level. In other words, an event patron located in a city suburb typically does not factor travel time into a decision to attend a professional or major college sporting event at a downtown venue.

Origin location analysis

An origin location analysis represents the most accurate method for developing an event-specific regional directional distribution. This analysis utilises a statistically significant database of event patron travel origins. Input data includes advance or season ticket holder place of residence (e.g., place or zip code) or place of trip origin obtained through a past/similar event travel survey. An event economic impact study also indicates the cities or regions patrons will arrive from.

A discrete/recurring event at a permanent venue requires ticket sales, and event organisers initiate ticket sales weeks and even months in advance of the event. But, event organisers or ticket sales companies may consider customer information confidential or proprietary. An event patron travel survey proves effective in determining the exact origin of a patron trip to a planned special event. For instance, weekday events may attract a significant percentage of non-home-based trips as event patrons arrive from work. A survey of patrons attending weeknight baseball games at Pacific Bell Park in San Francisco indicates 28 percent of patrons come from work. An event patron travel survey captures this critical information. Event patron departures from the event venue site typically involve home as a destination.

Practitioners performing an origin location analysis determine a geographical distribution of event patron origins. In turn, this distribution defines the freeway and arterial corridors that event patrons will use to access the event venue site in addition to a traffic distribution. An origin location analysis applies to all planned special events.

Parking Demand Analysis

A parking demand analysis functions to determine the amount of required parking for event patrons in the vicinity of the event venue. A parking occupancy study drives the overall analysis and determination of event parking areas. The level of parking spaces occupied, relative to lot capacity, at intermittent time intervals.

Figure 4 presents a parking demand analysis process used to determine the adequacy of event venue (on-site) parking and the identification of appropriate off-site parking areas. The flowchart denotes an analysis conducted for a one-time interval. Practitioners should perform an iterative parking demand analysis, over hourly time periods as necessary, if considering parking areas characterised by high background parking turnover.

Examination of on-site parking areas must account for spaces lost to the event sponsors, bus staging, limousine and taxi staging, media parking, event employee parking, and event participant parking. Net parking supply incorporates event staging needs and any background traffic that can legally use the parking area during event hours of operation. In order to conceptually measure parking supply within a non-striped area, assume 150 cars per acre as a rule of thumb. The travel forecast analysis yields an estimate of parking demand by quantifying the anticipated number of event-generated automobile trips. Aside from continuous events, practitioners should perform a parking demand analysis that accounts for maximum event-generated parking demand.

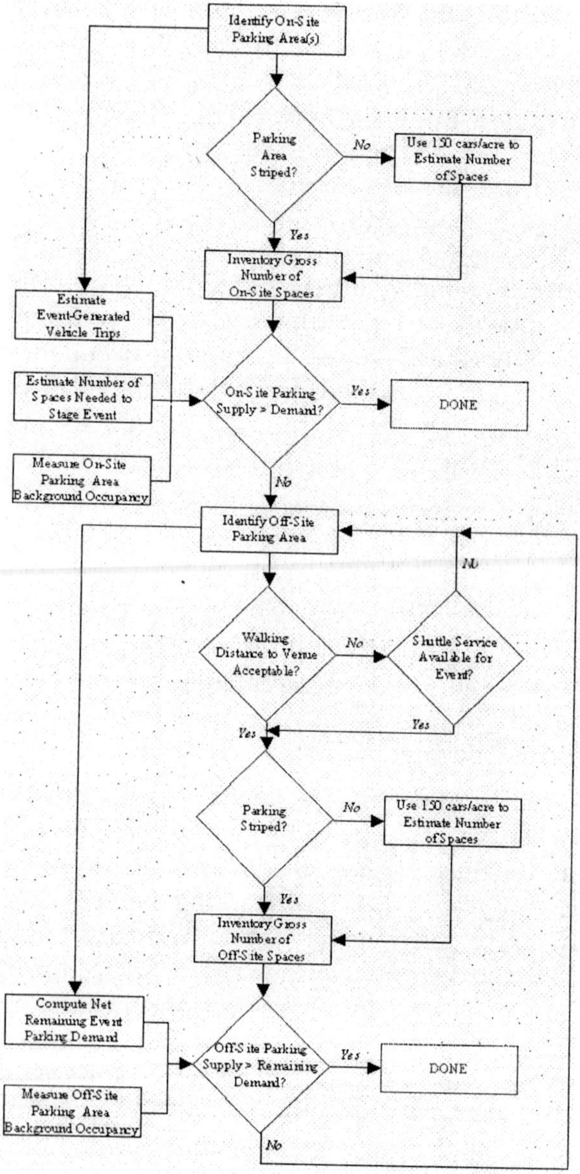

Figure 4. Parking Demand Analysis Process

In evaluating parking supply versus demand, consider as a rule of thumb that 90 to 95 percent lot occupancy represents a full parking area. This especially applies under scenarios where event patrons must self-park. When a parking area reaches a near-capacity occupancy level, drivers experience difficulty locating an empty parking space and must circulate through the lot again or seek another parking area. Continuous events and street use events often utilise self-park areas. Overflow parking areas comprise both on-street parking and public/ private off-street parking areas, located off-site but in the immediate vicinity of the event venue.

Traffic Demand Analysis

A traffic demand analysis determines: (1) a local area directional distribution and (2) the overall assignment of event-generated traffic. This analysis references results obtained through the travel forecast, market area analysis, and parking demand analysis. The local area directional distribution indicates freeway ramps and intersections, including turning movements, traversed by event-generated traffic arriving to or departing from a planned special event. The regional directional distribution, as determined in the market area analysis, quantifies the percentage of event patron trips by regional freeway and arterial corridor, and the planned special event parking areas, as determined in the parking demand analysis, represent sink nodes or location of trip destination.

Traffic assignment includes event-generated automobile traffic, express buses, charter buses, limousines, and other vehicles transporting event patrons, participants, and event employees. Practitioners performing traffic demand analyses should possess a personal knowledge of the roadway system surrounding an event venue in addition to existing traffic conditions.

A parking demand analysis assesses event parking sufficiency. The analysis does not define local traffic patterns to/from individual parking areas. Practitioners, instead, must gauge the utility associated with drivers choosing individual parking areas. The key components comprising this utility include driving time, parking cost, and walking time. The attractiveness of each lot varies by freeway or arterial corridor serving the event site, yet event patrons will accept a moderate increase in overall driving/walking time in exchange for a substantial parking cost savings.

The event planning team and traffic management team must recognise such driver behaviour and formulate the appropriate traffic flow routes and develop traffic management strategies to manage site access and circulation effectively. Traffic demand analysis includes developing composite background and event-generated traffic projections for all roadway system facilities serving the event venue. Composite traffic volumes expressed as an hourly rate meet roadway capacity analysis input requirements. These rates identify the peak hour capacity analysis periods during event patron arrival and/or departure.

Practitioners must adjust background traffic volumes to account for displaced and diverted traffic due to road closures required to stage the planned special event. These road closures alter traffic patterns to/from commercial trip generators, residential areas, and places of worship. Displaced background traffic assignment involves identifying the shortest path alternate route that has excess capacity.

As a preliminary step to assess the need to perform a detailed roadway capacity analysis, draw a circular screen line around the event venue site. Note each roadway segment intercepted by the screen line, and estimate the segment's capacity in each direction of travel.

Create a chart of hourly composite traffic volumes for each identified segment, and assess capacity deficiencies in both directions of travel.

Roadway Capacity Analysis

A roadway capacity analysis uses traffic demand analysis results to measure the impact of a proposed planned special event on roadway system operations. At the feasibility study level, a roadway capacity analysis references existing roadway facility operations and capacity. The analysis assumes pedestrian access management strategies will minimise pedestrian/vehicular conflicts, and parking area access points provide sufficient service flow rates through proper design. Regardless of capacity analysis outcome, pedestrian accommodation and parking management represent key considerations in a planned special event traffic management plan.

Roadway capacity analysis involves freeway segments, freeway junctions such as ramps and weaving areas, street segments, signalised intersections, and unsignalised intersections. To evaluate these facilities, practitioners can employ one of two approaches: (1) analyse section and point capacity or (2) analyse network operations

— The first approach pertains to applying Highway Capacity Manual (HCM) recommended capacity analysis methodologies to discrete locations in the study area. Practitioners determine roadway sections, freeway junctions, or intersections for analysis, then apply an appropriate HCM methodology to identify movement capacity constraints and measure operations level of service.

— The latter approach concerns utilising a computer traffic simulation model to identify bottleneck locations, or hot spots, and associated saturation flow rates. Practitioners scope the size and detail of the simulation model network, and the model works to reveal operational deficiencies.

Computer traffic simulation models provide seamless analysis of traffic operations across a network of roadway segments and intersections. This proves particularly useful in analysing a corridor of closely spaced traffic signals where signal coordination and vehicle spillback from adjacent intersections sharply impact traffic operations. Numerous macroscopic and microscopic simulation models exist, including the CORSIM microscopic computer traffic simulation model developed and supported by FHWA. CORSIM can interface component freeway (FRESIM) and arterial (NETSIM) simulation models.

Mitigation of Congestion and Safety Impacts

Mitigating anticipated planned special event impacts on travel represents the ultimate goal of conducting a feasibility study. The mitigation of congestion and potential safety impacts identified through a feasibility study requires development of a traffic management plan and complementing travel demand management strategies. In turn, practitioners can utilise the tools and techniques used to determine feasibility study results in order to evaluate various mitigation strategies and determine if the selected strategies adequately mitigate identified transportation system deficiencies.

5

Management of Street Use Events

A street use event occurs on a street requiring temporary closure. Table 1 indicates different types of planned special events classified as a street use event. This category includes events that occur in rural, urban, and metropolitan areas. Street use events generally occur in a city or downtown central business district; however, race events, motorcycle rallies, and dignitary motorcades may necessitate temporary closure of arterial streets or, to accommodate a motorcade, limited-access highways.

Table 1. Types of Street Use Events

Event Type
- Parades
- Marathons
- Bicycle races
- Grand Prix auto races
- Motorcycle rallies
- Dignitary motorcades

Planned special event permitting guidelines and restrictions typically influence event operations characteristics (e.g., location, street use event route, time of occurrence, etc.) and govern whether a traffic management plan can mitigate the transportation impact of a particular street use event. Table 2 lists key characteristics of a street use event.

Table 2. Distinguishing Operating Characteristics of a Street Use Event

Characteristic
- Occurrence on a roadway requiring temporary closure
- Specific starting and predictable ending times
- Capacity of spectator viewing area not known
- Spectators not charged or ticketed
- Dedicated parking facilities not available

Special Considerations

In light of the characteristics of a street use event, special considerations when planning such an event include:

— Daily attendance, a key input in the travel forecast analysis process, is often difficult to estimate, and day-of-event weather conditions significantly affect it.

— The entire parade or race route represents the event venue.

— Parking areas and traffic flow routes serve an expanded site area.

— Race events or motorcycle rallies often require the temporary closure of roadways over a significant distance.

— Spectator viewing areas may have limited access to transit stations and adjacent high-capacity arterial roadways and freeways.

— High attendance events in downtown areas require extensive planning for parking and travel demand management.

— Major street use events typically generate trips from a multi-county region.

— These events impact parking and access required by nearby neighborhood residents and businesses.

— Temporary road closures, required to stage the event, impact background traffic and transit flow in addition to emergency vehicle access and other local services.

Event Planning

Since street use events take place on the roadway system and different event types have contrasting characteristics (e.g., parades versus road races), the event planning team should develop:

1. A feasibility study,
2. A traffic management plan, and
3. Travel demand management initiatives (as necessary).

The stakeholder composition of an event planning team varies by event, as most parades represent community events while road races and motorcycle rallies may involve commercial dealings.

In regard to a community-sponsored special event, transportation and/or law enforcement agencies usually bear the responsibility of developing all of the necessary event planning phase products. These stakeholders guide the planning process for commercial street use events as well. Jurisdictions may mandate that private event organisers use a standard route and adhere to numerous guidelines and regulations developed by public agencies, in the program planning phase, as part of a greater permit programme for all planned special events.

Recurring street use events, such as an annual holiday parade, allow stakeholders to reference a past feasibility study and traffic management plan, coupled with operations successes and lessons learned, when conducting advance planning activities for a future event. However, due to the significant time between recurring street use events, the event planning team must anticipate

— changes in the operations characteristics of a future event,

— modifications to the transportation system serving the event, and

— changes in the community (e.g., land use, socioeconomic, regulations, etc.).

Figure 1 presents 31 steps in the event operations planning process for all planned special events. The flowchart covers development and integration of the phase's aforementioned three products. In turn, practitioners can use example applications presented for a street use event to manage travel for other categories of planned special events.

Steps for Infrequent Events

The flowchart in Figure 1 represents a suggested order of event operations planning activities. However, as noted below, the event planning team can modify activities to create a dynamic and more effective planning process tailored to the scope of a specific planned special event:

— A jurisdiction planned special event permit process and requirements will scope, schedule, and direct event operations planning activities for street use events.

— The event planning team should plan an event route, spectator traffic flow routes, and background traffic accommodation strategies early in the event operations planning phase, referencing guidelines and tactics for developing a traffic flow plan.

— Links between process steps are two-way as stakeholders evaluate alternative strategies and/or integrate traffic management plan components.

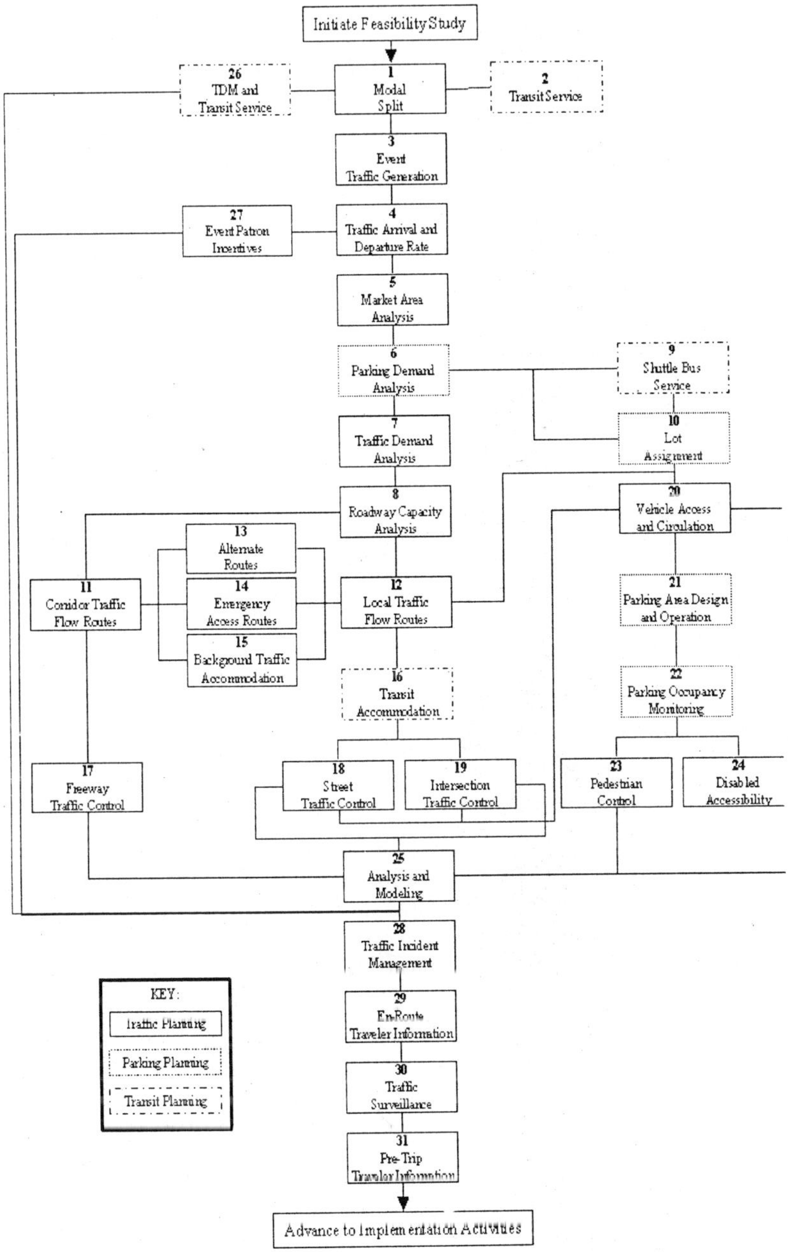

Figure 1. Event Operations Planning Process Flowchart

— The event planning team can develop different traffic management plan components concurrently.

Implementation Event Activities

Implementation activities represent an essential phase in advance planning for street use events. The traffic management team may involve new interagency relationships, and it requires an event-specific implementation plan to communicate specifics of the new traffic management plan prepared by the event planning team.

Because particular street use event types occur infrequently, stakeholder simulation exercises prove valuable in assisting traffic management team personnel understand the roles and responsibilities of participating stakeholders in addition to the actions taken on the day-of-event.

Equipment testing marks another key consideration as day-of-event operations at and in the vicinity of the event site usually depend on portable equipment for traffic control, surveillance, and dissemination of en-route traveller information. These intensive stakeholder activities reflect the typical unfamiliarity with managing travel for a street use event coupled with the fact that transportation management activities, on the order required for a planned special event, may not regularly take place in the vicinity of the event site.

Table 2 presents a checklist of implementation and day-of-event activities for stakeholders to consider regarding any street use event. As indicated in the table, the event planning team must determine, based on various event operations characteristics (e.g., event type, event location, event time of occurrence, attendance, market area, etc.) and other external factors, what unique set of activities apply in handling a specific special event.

Table 2. Implementation and Day-of-Event Activities for Street Use Events

Action
- Develop an implementation plan. - Conduct a stakeholder simulation exercise(s). - Test equipment resources slated for use on the day-of-event. - Recruit and train volunteers to fulfill personnel resource needs. - Implement a traffic management team management process. - Designate a multi-agency command post. - Conduct traffic management plan evaluation(s) during the day-of-event. - Establish protocol for traffic management team officials to consider and implement changes to the traffic management plan to accommodate real-time traffic conditions. - Establish interagency communication protocol. - Review communication equipment compatibility. - Use the media to communicate with event patrons and other transportation users. - Perform traffic monitoring on the day-of-event.

Some distinguishing considerations of this event category during the day-of-event activities phase include:

— Street use events demand the use of experienced personnel in the field on the day-of-event. Law enforcement officers or other personnel properly trained in traffic control should (1) direct traffic at intersections adjacent to closed streets and (2) control pedestrian crossing locations.

— Supplementing traffic management team personnel with temporary staff and volunteers may represent a necessary action to meet staffing requirements. Competent adult volunteers can monitor barricade placement and minor intersection/driveway approaches. Many volunteers have no past experience in tasks associated with traffic and pedestrian control and parking operations. As a result, volunteer training becomes paramount to the success of day-of-event operations.

— The traffic management team likely includes stakeholder representatives involved in managing travel for a particular street use event type for the first time. To ensure successful traffic management plan deployment, the traffic management team must adopt a formal management process and establish an interagency communication structure and protocol to support day-of-event operations.

— Other essential team management considerations involve (1) the designation of an Incident Commander for the planned special event and (2) the set up of a temporary, multi-agency command post at or near the event site.

— Traffic management team officials should anticipate enacting modifications to the traffic management plan during the street use event.

— Surveillance information and performance evaluation data define transportation operation conditions and, thus, influence decision-making at a day-of-event briefing.

— Due to the challenge of estimating event-generated traffic in the event feasibility study, day-of-event briefings should occur at frequent intervals during event ingress operations. Moreover, traffic management team officials should conduct an expanded briefing prior to the end of the event in order to reassess the traffic management and implementation plan for egress operations, taking into consideration traffic and pedestrian demand observed during ingress in addition to traffic and transit operations on alternate routes.

— The collection and evaluation of transportation system performance data proves valuable in guiding decision-making not only on the day-of-event but also for recurring street use events (e.g., annual parades or street races). Stakeholders can archive raw data for use in future feasibility studies, and various evaluation measures can identify specific areas that require improvement for future, similar events using the same route.

— The traffic management team must exercise great care in collecting performance evaluation data in order to ensure data quality and consistency.

Post-Event Activities

All of the primary products of this phase, particularly participant evaluations and post-event debriefings, apply to evaluating transportation operations for street use events. Given the infrequent occurrence of street use events coupled with the scarcity of travel forecast data, post-event activity results represent a key resource in planning for future street use events in a region. Table 3 presents a checklist of post-event activities for street use events.

Some distinguishing considerations of this event category during the post-event activities phase include:

— In regard to participant evaluation, street use event patron travel surveys yield important information and statistics that can assist practitioners in (1) improving the accuracy of future street use event travel forecasts and (2) developing travel demand management incentives (e.g., public transit incentives and express/charter bus services) for similar events.

Table 3. Post-Event Activities for Street Use Events

Action
- Review measures of effectiveness identified in event operations planning phase. - Compile agency measures of effectiveness. - Compile performance evaluation data. - Conduct stakeholder participant debriefing. - Conduct event patron survey. - Conduct public survey. - Conduct a post-event debriefing meeting. - Prepare a post-event report.

— Periodic public surveys warrant consideration for special events under this category as event performance evaluation data fails to assess all community impacts. Survey results alert special event stakeholders of impacts to affected residents and businesses, in addition to non-attendee transportation system users, that may continue to occur with each successive special event on a particular route. As a result, stakeholders can develop and implement appropriate strategies (e.g., create/revise a standard street use event route, revise alternate route plans, etc.) and regulations to mitigate the identified impact(s) for future planned special events.

— Post-event debriefings represent a common and recommended stakeholder activity for street use events.

— On a regional level, such meetings may coincide with a regular traffic incident management team meeting.

— A key aspect of a post-event debriefing for street use events involves preparing detailed meeting minutes that include the identification of key successes and lessons learned. In turn, findings may refine special event permit programme provisions for future street use events.

— Considering the potential significant time between similar event types, stakeholders must chronicle participant survey results and debriefing meetings so that those stakeholders charged with managing travel for future street use events can tap the wisdom of past participants.

— The occurrence of a major, recurring street use event warrants development or update of a post-event report. In turn, the report can serve as a working document to assist in advance planning for the next (year's) event.

— A post-event report for a recurring street use event should include an operational cost analysis to assist stakeholders in identifying potential cost-saving resource deployment strategies for the next event occurrence.

Programme Planning Activities

Programme planning activities involve the development of policies, programmes, and initiatives that facilitate improved planning and management of travel for future planned special events. Programme planning for street use events include activities, as summarised in Table 4, on both a regional and local level.

Table 4. Programme Planning Activities for Street Use Events

Product	Topic
Institutional frameworks	- Creation of a regional transportation committee on planned special events (e.g., oversight team). - Development of a formal planned special event permit programme.

	- Creation of a transportation operations task force for a recurring street use event. - Development of a joint operations policy.
Policies and regulations	- Traffic and parking restrictions. - Standard street use event routes . - Public-private towing agreements.
Infrastructure deployment	- Advanced parking management system. - Electronic fee collection system. - Planned alternate route for diverting background traffic around a venue. - Portable traffic management system. - Express, charter or shuttle bus service. - Telephone information systems. - Public information campaign.

Some distinguishing considerations of this event category during the programme planning phase include:

— A regional transportation committee on planned special events considers the planning and resource requirements of street use events in connection with managing all planned special events in a region. A primary committee focus concerns facilitating interagency coordination and collaboration. For instance, a task force may exist for a specific large-scale, recurring street use event that works throughout the year to integrate past event successes and lessons learned into future event planning.

— Two or more stakeholders, representing multiple jurisdictions and/or disciplines, may establish a joint operations policy for managing travel for all planned special events in a region.

— Stakeholders may develop a standard route for all street use events of a certain type (e.g., parades, street races, etc.) that occur within a region or jurisdiction in order to create a more efficient event operations planning process for future street use events.

— Because street use events occur infrequently and on the roadway system, an infrastructure needs assessment on the programme planning level should focus on equipment and technology applications transferable to managing all planned special events in a region and/or day-to-day transportation system operations.

— A planned special event permit programme proves particularly effective for street use events that, because of such characteristics as event attendance, event time of occurrence, and event location (e.g., route), may (1) conflict with municipal or state guidelines and regulations and (2) impact transportation operations and the community. The programme specifies a permit process, coupled with supporting restrictions and requirements, that allows stakeholders to plan and assess all types of street use events within a common framework. For instance, stakeholder review of a proposed event route represents one step in the permit process in addition to a key decision criteria for rendering permit application approval.

Funding represents a key public agency consideration for street use events in the programme planning phase.

— Commercial events may involve event organisers and participants from outside the community hosting the event.

— Prior to initiating event operations planning activities for a specific street use event, stakeholders should establish a funding mechanism for recovering costs incurred in providing services during the event operations planning phase and resources on the day-of-event.

— Funding often represents a requirement of a comprehensive planned special event permit programme.

6

GUIDELINES FOR CONTINUOUS EVENT MANAGEMENT

There are different types of planned special events classified as a continuous event.

— Fairs.

– Festivals.

— Conventions and expos.

— Air and automobile shows.

This category includes events that occur in urban and metropolitan areas, and the rural event category includes continuous events that take place in rural areas. Aside from conventions and state/county fairs, many continuous events take place at a temporary venue, a park, or other large open space. These venues host planned special events on a less frequent basis than permanent multi-use venues, and planned special event permitting typically governs whether a temporary venue can adequately handle the transportation impact of a particular continuous event. The key characteristics of a continuous event are follows:

— Occurrence often over multiple days.

— Arrival and departure of event patrons throughout the event day.

— Typically little or no advance ticket sales.
— Capacity of venue not always known.
— Occurrence sometimes at temporary venues.

Special Considerations

In light of the characteristics of a continuous event, special considerations when planning such an event include:

— Daily attendance, a key input in the travel forecast analysis process, is often difficult to estimate, and day-of-event weather conditions may significantly affect it.

— The traffic generation characteristics and market area of different continuous events may vary considerably, thus limiting the transfer of historical data between non-identical special events.

— Most events do not have an attendance capacity or defined "sell-out."

— Venues may have limited access to transit stations and adjacent high-capacity arterial roadways and freeways.

— High attendance events in downtown areas require extensive planning for parking and travel demand management.

— Major continuous events typically generate trips from a multi-county region.

— Potential weather impacts require the consideration of a wide range of contingency plans relative to site access, parking, pedestrian access, traffic control, and traffic incident management.

— Continuous events held at temporary venues may significantly impact nearby neighborhood residents and businesses.

Continuous Event Planning

Because of the contrasting characteristics of different continuous events and the respective venues hosting these events, the event planning team should develop

1. A feasibility study,
2. A traffic management plan, and
3. Travel demand management initiatives (as necessary) in the event operations planning phase.

The stakeholder composition of an event planning team varies by event, as some continuous events represent community or not-for-profit events while others involve commercial dealings. Recurring continuous events, such as an annual fair or air show, permit stakeholders to reference a past feasibility study and traffic management plan, coupled with operations successes and lessons learned, when conducting advance planning activities for a future event.

However, due to the significant time between recurring continuous events, the event planning team must anticipate:

1. Changes in the operations characteristics of a future event,
2. Modifications to the transportation system serving the event, and
3. Changes in the community (e.g., land use, socioeconomic, regulations, etc.).

The event planning team can modify activities to create a dynamic and more effective planning process tailored to the scope of a specific planned special event:

— A jurisdiction planned special event permit process and requirements will scope, schedule, and direct event operations planning activities for continuous events.

— Links between process steps are two-way as stakeholders evaluate alternative strategies and/or integrate traffic management plan components.

— The event planning team can develop different traffic management plan components concurrently.

When following the process, practitioners should review:

— Advance planning and travel management process and considerations as appropriate, for continuous events that occur at a permanent venue (e.g., stadium, arena, amphitheater, and convention center).

— Important advance planning considerations and external factors, that influence planning activitics. For instance, effective and rapid stakeholder review of event operations planning products requires:

  — an annotated planning timeline,

  — a review process, and

  — performance standards.

Implementation Activities

Implementation activities represent an essential phase in advance planning for continuous events. The traffic management team involves new interagency relationships, and it requires an event-specific implementation plan to communicate specifics of the new traffic management plan prepared by the event planning team.

Because particular continuous event types occur infrequently, stakeholder simulation exercises prove valuable in assisting traffic management team personnel understand the roles and responsibilities of participating stakeholders in addition to the actions taken on the day-of-event.

Equipment testing marks another key consideration.

These intensive stakeholder activities reflect the typical unfamiliarity with managing travel for a continuous event coupled with the fact that transportation management activities, on the order required for a planned special event, may not regularly take place in the vicinity of the event venue.

Table 1 presents an implementation and day-of-event activities for stakeholders to consider regarding any continuous event. As indicated in the table, the event planning team must determine, based on various event operations characteristics (e.g., event type, event location, event time of occurrence, attendance, market area, etc.) and other external factors, what unique set of activities apply in handling a specific special event.

Table 1. Implementation and Day-of-Event Activities for Continuous Events

Applies
- Develop an implementation plan. - Conduct a stakeholder simulation exercise(s). - Test equipment resources slated for use on the day-of-event. - Recruit and train volunteers to fulfill personnel resource needs. - Implement a traffic management team management process. - Designate a multi-agency command post. - Conduct a traffic management plan evaluation(s) during the day-of-event. - Establish protocol for traffic management team officials to consider and implement changes to the traffic management plan to accommodate real-time traffic conditions. - Establish interagency communication protocol. - Review communication equipment compatibility. - Use the media to communicate with event patrons and other transportation users. - Perform traffic monitoring on the day-of-event.

Some distinguishing considerations of this event category during the day-of-event activities phase include:

— The scope and duration of continuous events, especially those that occur over multiple days, demand a significant level of personnel resources. Supplementing traffic management team personnel with temporary staff and volunteers may represent a necessary action to meet daily staffing requirements. However, many volunteers have no past experience in tasks associated with traffic and pedestrian control and parking operations. As a result, volunteer training becomes paramount to the success of day-of-event operations.

— The traffic management team likely includes stakeholder representatives involved in managing travel for a particular continuous event type for the first time. To ensure successful traffic management plan deployment, the traffic management team must adopt a formal management process and establish an interagency communication structure and protocol to support day-of-event operations.

— Other essential team management considerations involve (1) the designation of an Incident Commander for the planned special event and (2) the set up of a temporary, multi-agency command post at or near the event venue.

— Traffic management team officials should anticipate enacting modifications to the traffic management plan throughout the duration of the continuous event.

— Surveillance information and performance evaluation data define transportation operation conditions and, thus, influence decision-making at a day-of-event briefing.

— Multi-day continuous events should include: (1) a traffic management team meeting at the end of each day's activities to review the traffic management plan and team performance and/or (2) a traffic management team meeting before the start of the next event day.

— The collection and evaluation of transportation system performance data proves valuable in guiding decision-making not only on the day-of-event but also for recurring continuous events. Stakeholders can archive raw data for use in future feasibility studies, and various evaluation measures can identify specific areas that require improvement for future, similar events at the subject venue.

— The traffic management team must exercise great care in collecting performance evaluation data in order to ensure data quality and consistency.

Post-Event Activities

All of the primary products of this phase (e.g., participant evaluation, post-event debriefing, and post-event report) have a high level of applicability to continuous events. Given the infrequent occurrence of continuous events coupled with the scarcity of travel forecast data, post-event activity results represent a key resource in planning for future continuous events in a region.

Some distinguishing considerations of this event category during the post-event activities phase include:

— In regard to participant evaluation, continuous event patron travel surveys yield important information and statistics that can assist practitioners in (1) improving the accuracy of future continuous event travel forecasts and (2) developing travel demand management incentives (e.g., public transit incentives and express/charter bus services) for similar events.

— Periodic public surveys warrant consideration for special events under this category as event performance evaluation data fails to assess all community impacts. Survey results alert special event stakeholders of impacts to affected residents and businesses, in addition to non-attendee transportation system users, that may continue to occur with each successive special event at a particular venue location. As a result, stakeholders can develop and implement appropriate strategies (e.g., enforcement, etc.) to mitigate the identified impact(s) for future planned special events.

— Post-event debriefings represent a common and recommended stakeholder activity for continuous events.

— On a regional level, such meetings may coincide with a regular traffic incident management team meeting.

— A key aspect of a post-event debriefing for continuous events involves preparing detailed meeting minutes that include the identification of key successes and lessons learned.

— Considering the potential significant time between similar event types, stakeholders must chronicle participant survey results and debriefing meetings so that those stakeholders charged with managing travel for future continuous events can tap the wisdom of past participants.

— The occurrence of a major, recurring continuous event warrants development of a post-event report. In turn, the report can serve as a working document to assist in advance planning for the next (year's) event.

— A post-event report for a recurring continuous event should include an operational cost analysis to assist stakeholders in identifying potential cost-saving resource deployment strategies for the next event occurrence.

Programme Planning Activities

Programme planning activities involve the development of policies, programmes, and initiatives that facilitate improved planning and management of travel for future planned special events.

Some distinguishing considerations of this event category during the programme planning phase include:

— A regional transportation committee on planned special events considers the planning and resource requirements of continuous events in connection with managing all planned special events in a region. A primary committee focus concerns facilitating interagency coordination and collaboration. For instance, a task force may exist for a specific large-scale, recurring continuous event that works throughout the year to integrate past event successes and lessons learned into future event planning.

— Two or more stakeholders, representing multiple jurisdictions and/or disciplines, may establish a joint operations policy for managing travel for all planned special events in a region.

— Because continuous events occur infrequently and occasionally at temporary venues, an infrastructure needs assessment on the programme planning level should focus on equipment and technology applications transferable to managing all planned special events in a region and/or day-to-day transportation system operations.

— A planned special event permit programme proves particularly effective for continuous events that, because of such characteristics as event attendance and event location, may (1) conflict with municipal or state guidelines and regulations and (2) impact transportation operations and the community. The programme specifies a permit process, coupled with supporting restrictions and requirements, that allows stakeholders to plan and assess all types of continuous events within a common framework.

— Funding represents a key public agency consideration for continuous events in the programme planning phase.

— Commercial events may involve event organisers and participants from outside the community hosting the event.

— Prior to initiating event operations planning activities for a specific continuous event, stakeholders should establish a funding mechanism for recovering costs incurred in providing services during the event operations planning phase and resources on the day-of-event.

— Funding often represents a requirement of a comprehensive planned special event permit programme.

7

Management of Multi-Venue Events

A multi-venue event refers to multiple planned special events that occur within a region at or near the same time. Individual events may differ by classification category. Concurrent planned special events require consideration as a multi-venue event if traffic generated by different, competing special events use the same traffic flow routes (e.g., freeway/arterial corridors, local streets) or parking areas over the same time frame. As a result, stakeholders involved in planning and managing individual special events must, as a group, forecast and mitigate the global impact of concurrent special events on transportation system operations.

Types of Multi-Venue Events

- Occurrence of a single-theme event requiring multiple venues to stage the event.
- Occurrence of a downtown parade or festival in the vicinity of a downtown fixed venue also hosting a special event.
- Occurrence of special events at two fixed venues in a region at or near the same time.

Characteristics of a Multi-Venue Event

— Occurrence of events at multiple venues and at or near the same time.

— Events having a time specific duration, a continuous duration, or both.

— Overall capacity generally not known if continuous events or street use events are involved.

In light of the characteristics of a multi-venue event, special considerations when planning such an event include:

— Traffic flow routes to/from different events may use the same road segments, and predominant traffic demand occurs in the same or opposite directions.

— Traffic flow routes that serve different special event venues may intersect.

— Overflow parking areas typically reserved for a recurring special event or permanent venue may be required to accommodate demand from nearby concurrent events.

— Ingress and egress operations for concurrent events may occur at the same time.

— Event patrons and participants may travel from one planned special event to another.

— Traffic control and traveller information for different special events can confuse event patrons.

Planning

Planned multi-venue events include, for example, multi-day sporting games (e.g., Olympic style) that require multiple venues to stage various events and major fireworks displays in areas offering several vantage points (e.g., parks, etc.) spread out over a large area. Other multi-venue events evolve as a result of individual planned special events slated to occur within a region at or near the same time. These events involve any combination of discrete/recurring events at a permanent venue, continuous events, and street use events. As a result, the collective multi-venue event often represents a one-time occurrence, particularly if one or more individual events involve a sporting or concert event.

Concurrent events may span one day or multiple days. The scope and infrequent occurrence of a multi-venue event generally requires the event planning team(s) to develop:

— a feasibility study,

— a traffic management plan, and

— travel demand management initiatives (as necessary) in the event operations planning phase.

The overall event operations planning approach for a multi-venue event remains the same for all event types. That is, the event planning team should first develop preliminary event operations products on a venue-by-venue basis and then combine and evaluate venue-specific findings and recommended mitigation actions for the multi-venue event. The latter step helps to determine:

— additional transportation system capacity constraints not identified in individual event/venue analyses,

— potential conflicts in event/venue traffic management plan provisions, and

— additional mitigation measures designed to improve transportation operations for the overall multi-venue event.

A multi-venue event places an emphasis on interagency coordination and collaboration. Each venue event may involve a distinct group of planning and operations stakeholders if individual events within a region do not relate to each other. Event operations planning for a multi-venue event requires input and participation by all involved stakeholder groups. Public agency stakeholders responsible for the planning or approval of individual venue events should facilitate interaction between event planning teams and ensure mitigation of transportation and community impacts from the composite multi-venue event.

However, as noted below, the event planning team can modify activities to create a dynamic and more effective planning process tailored to the scope of a specific planned special event:

— The event planning team should repeat process steps for individual venue events comprising the multi-venue event.

— Final planning products should account for the overall impact of the multi-venue event.

— Links between process steps are two-way as stakeholders evaluate alternative strategies and/or integrate traffic management plan components.

— The event planning team can develop different traffic management plan components concurrently.

Implementation and Day-of-Event Activities

Implementation activities represent an essential phase in advance planning for multi-venue events. Depending on event type, one traffic management team may handle day-of-event operations for multiple venues (e.g., sporting games) or a single venue. Nonetheless, implementation plans for individual event venues must correlate in terms of traffic control strategies deployed and resources used. Such specifications can be organised through matrices for easy reference. Because multi-venue events occur infrequently, stakeholder simulation exercises prove valuable in assisting traffic management team supervisors and field personnel understand the roles and responsibilities of participating stakeholders in addition to the operations game plan and actions for individual venue events.

Tabletop exercises allow traffic management team officials to review the impact of certain event-specific action plans on other concurrent events. A full-scale simulation proves advantageous by providing venue managers and transportation operators, stationed at various command posts (e.g., on-site and at the transportation management center), with the opportunity to test the communications infrastructure used on the day-of-event. These intensive stakeholder activities reflect the typical unfamiliarity with managing travel for a multi-venue event coupled with the fact that transportation management activities usually performed for a particular, recurring special event may require modification to accommodate nearby concurrent planned special events.

The event planning team must determine, based on various event operations characteristics (e.g., event type, event location, event time of occurrence, attendance, market area, etc.) and other external factors, what unique set of activities apply in handling all venue events comprising a multi-venue special event.

Some distinguishing considerations of this event category during the day-of-event activities phase include:

— The scope of multi-venue events demand a significant level of personnel resources. Supplementing traffic management team personnel with temporary staff and volunteers may represent a necessary action to meet staffing requirements for all concurrent special events.

Many volunteers have no past experience in tasks associated with traffic and pedestrian control and parking operations. As a result, volunteer training becomes paramount to the success of day-of-event operations.

— Multi-venue events may strain available stakeholder resources needed to manage travel in the vicinity of a particular event venue; therefore, traffic management team officials should reconfirm the availability of necessary traffic control and communications equipment prior to the day-of-event.

— To ensure successful traffic management plan deployment and coordination across all venue locations, the traffic management team(s) must establish an interagency communication structure and protocol to support multi-venue event operations on the day-of-event.

— Other essential team management considerations involve the set up of a command post, most likely at a regional transportation management center, for monitoring and managing all venue events.

— Traffic management team officials should anticipate enacting modifications to the traffic management plan(s) during the multi-venue event.

— Surveillance information and performance evaluation data define transportation operation conditions and, thus, influence decision-making at a day-of-event briefing.

— Day-of-event briefings should occur at key breakpoints, such as at the end of ingress/egress operations for a particular venue event, during a multi-venue event. This allows traffic management team officials to reassess the traffic management and implementation plan for all concurrent events and make revisions as necessary.

Post-Event Activities

Some distinguishing considerations of this event category during the post-event activities phase include:

— With regard to multi-venue events consisting of individual non-related venue events occurring at or near the same time, stakeholders may conduct post-event activities specific to individual events.

— Post-event debriefings represent a common and recommended stakeholder activity for all multi-venue events.

a) On a regional level, such meetings may coincide with a regular traffic incident management team meeting.

b) The meeting agenda should include discussion topics on the planning process, interagency communication, and coordination of travel management activities among individual venue events on the day-of-event.

c) A key aspect of a post-event debriefing for multi-venue events involves preparing detailed meeting minutes that include the identification of key successes and lessons learned.

d) Considering the potential significant time between multi-venue events, stakeholders must chronicle debriefing meetings so that those stakeholders charged with managing travel for future events can tap the wisdom of past participants.

— The occurrence of a major, single-theme multi-venue event warrants participant evaluations and the development of a post-event report. Given the infrequent occurrence of this event type, post-event activity results represent a key resource in planning for the next event occurrence either in the host region or another locale (e.g., for roving multi-venue events).

Planning and Management of Programmes

Programme planning activities involve the development of policies, programmes, and initiatives that facilitate improved planning and management of travel for future planned special events. Programme planning for multi-venue events include activities, as summarised in Table 1, aimed at facilitating interagency coordination both during the event operations planning phase and on the day-of-event when concurrent venue events take place.

Table 1. Programme Planning Activities for Multi-Venue Events

Product	Topic
Institutional frameworks	Creation of a regional transportation committee on planned special events (e.g., oversight team).
	Development of a formal planned special event permit programme.
	Creation of a transportation operations task force for a multi-venue event.
	Development of a joint operations policy.
	Development of a mutual-aid agreement to facilitate resource sharing.

Some distinguishing considerations of this event category during the programme planning phase include:

— A regional transportation committee on planned special events considers the planning and resource requirements of multi-venue events in connection with managing all planned special events in a region. A primary committee focus concerns facilitating interagency coordination and collaboration. For instance, the committee may form a task force if stakeholders expect that multiple venue events will impact the same traffic flow routes and/or parking areas over the same time frame, thus requiring planning and operation as a multi-venue event.

— Two or more stakeholders, representing multiple jurisdictions and/or disciplines, may establish a joint operations policy to ensure a cooperative effort in managing travel for all planned special events in a region.

— Stakeholders may develop a mutual-aid agreement to facilitate resource sharing and/or reimbursement for services in order to handle future planned special events, particularly events under this category.

— A planned special event permit programme proves particularly effective for multi-venue events that, because of such characteristics as event attendance, event times of occurrence, and event locations may (1) conflict with municipal or state guidelines and regulations and (2) impact transportation operations and the community. For instance, permit regulations may restrict the approval of a particular planned special event if it conflicts with another planned special event.

— Funding represents a key public agency consideration for multi-venue events in the programme planning phase.

a) Commercial events may involve event organisers and participants from outside the community hosting the event.

b) Prior to initiating event operations planning activities for a specific multi-venue event, stakeholders should establish a funding mechanism for recovering costs incurred in providing services during the event operations planning phase and resources on the day-of-event.

c) Funding often represents a requirement of a comprehensive planned special event permit programme.

8

Management of Rural Events

A rural event encompasses any discrete/recurring event or continuous event that occurs in a rural area. Folloeing are different types of rural events:

— Fairs and festivals in rural areas

— Events at a rural amphitheater

— Events at a rural race track venue

— Professional golf tournaments in rural areas

Characteristics of rural event are:

— Rural or rural/tourist area

— High attendance events attracting event patrons from a regional area

— Limited roadway capacity serving an event venue

— Area lacking regular transit service

— Events having either a time specific duration or continuous duration

In light of the characteristics of a rural event, special considerations when planning such an event include:

— Need for stakeholders to assume new and/or expanded roles.

— Need to work closely with all affected stakeholders in order:

a) to gain their help in identifying concerns and

b) to introduce them to mitigation measures that they may be unfamiliar with due to the rural nature of the area.

— Need to work closely with involved stakeholders so that a trust relationship is established, thus lessening sensitive feelings of an outsider coming in and imposing initiatives that could overlook the significance of local issues.

— Existence of limited road capacity to access the event venue and potentially limited parking capacity at the venue.

— Existence of fewer alternate routes to accommodate event and background traffic.

— Lack of regular transit service and hotels near the venue.

— Existence of limited or no permanent infrastructure for monitoring and managing traffic.

— Generation of trips from a multi-county region.

Event Planning

The scope and infrequent/one-time occurrence of a high-attendance rural event, coupled with the typical limited capacity of transportation systems in rural areas, requires the event planning team to develop:

— a feasibility study,

— a traffic management plan, and

— travel demand management initiatives (as necessary) in the event operations planning phase.

The stakeholder composition of an event planning team varies by event, as some rural events represent community or not-for-profit events while others involve commercial dealings. In regard to a community-sponsored special event, transportation and/or law enforcement agencies usually bear the responsibility of developing all of the necessary event planning phase products. Recurring rural events, such as an annual festival or auto race, permit stakeholders to reference a past feasibility study and traffic management plan, coupled with operations successes and lessons learned, when conducting advance planning activities for a future event.

However, due to the significant time between recurring rural events, the event planning team must anticipate

— changes in the operations characteristics of a future event,
— modifications to the transportation system serving the event, and
— changes in the community (e.g., land use, socioeconomic, regulations, etc.).

However, as noted below, the event planning team can modify activities to create a dynamic and more effective planning process tailored to the scope of a specific planned special event:

— A jurisdiction planned special event permit process and requirements will scope, schedule, and direct event operations planning activities for rural events, particularly continuous events occurring in rural areas.
— Based on lessons learned from past special events at a particular permanent venue, stakeholders may programme new infrastructure or adopt new policies (e.g., parking restrictions) early in the event operations planning process.
— Links between process steps are two-way as stakeholders evaluate alternative strategies and/or integrate traffic management plan components.

— The event planning team can develop different traffic management plan components concurrently.

Implementation Activities

Implementation activities represent an essential phase in advance planning for rural events. The traffic management team may involve new interagency relationships, and it requires an event-specific implementation plan to communicate specifics of the new traffic management plan prepared by the event planning team. Because particular rural event types occur infrequently, stakeholder simulation exercises prove valuable in assisting traffic management team personnel understand the roles and responsibilities of participating stakeholders in addition to the actions taken on the day-of-event.

Exercises must involve field staff, some of whom represent personnel obtained temporarily from other regions for the purpose of increasing local stakeholder (e.g., state police, etc.) staff for an event. Temporary staff, although possibly experienced in traffic control, usually do not have familiarity with the local transportation system or roadways in the vicinity of the venue site. Equipment testing marks another key consideration as day-of-event operations at and in the vicinity of the event site usually depend on portable equipment for traffic control, surveillance, and dissemination of en-route traveler information. These intensive stakeholder activities reflect the typical unfamiliarity with managing travel for a rural event coupled with the fact that transportation management activities, on the order required for a planned special event, may not regularly take place in the vicinity of the event site.

Some distinguishing considerations of the event category during the day-of-event activities phase include:

— The scope of high-attendance rural events demand personnel resources that may exceed the level of available staff from local event stakeholders. Supplementing traffic management team personnel with temporary staff and volunteers may represent a necessary action to meet staffing requirements for rural special events. Many volunteers have no past experience in tasks associated with traffic and pedestrian control and parking operations. As a result, volunteer training becomes paramount to the success of day-of-event operations.

— The traffic management team likely includes stakeholder representatives involved in managing travel for a particular rural event type for the first time. To ensure successful traffic management plan deployment, the traffic management team must adopt a formal management process and establish an interagency communication structure and protocol to support day-of-event operations.

— Other essential team management considerations involve (1) the designation of an Incident Commander for the planned special event and (2) the set up of a temporary, multi-agency command post at or near the event venue.

— Traffic management team officials should anticipate enacting modifications to the traffic management plan during the rural event.

— Surveillance information and performance evaluation data define transportation operation conditions and, thus, influence decision-making at a day-of-event briefing. Given the typical lack of transportation management centers in rural areas, transportation system operators usually monitor system operations from the event command post using portable equipment (e.g., laptop computers, devices using radio/cellular/spread spectrum radio communication, etc.).

— The collection and evaluation of transportation system performance data proves valuable in guiding decision-making not only on the day-of-event but also for recurring rural events. Stakeholders can archive raw data for use in future feasibility studies, and various evaluation measures can identify specific areas that require improvement for future, similar events.

— The traffic management team must exercise great care in collecting performance evaluation data in order to ensure data quality and consistency.

Post-Event Activities

All of the primary products of this phase (e.g., participant evaluation, post-event debriefing, and post-event report) have a high level of applicability to rural events. Given the infrequent occurrence of rural events coupled with the scarcity of travel forecast data, post-event activity results represent a key resource in planning for future rural events in a region.

Some distinguishing considerations of this event category during the post-event activities phase include:

— In regard to participant evaluation, rural event patron travel surveys yield important information and statistics that can assist practitioners in (1) improving the accuracy of future rural event travel forecasts and (2) developing travel demand management incentives (e.g., express/charter bus services, event patron incentives) for the market area served by rural events.

— Periodic public surveys warrant consideration for special events under this category as event performance evaluation data fails to assess all community impacts. Survey results alert special event stakeholders of impacts to affected residents and businesses, in addition to non-attendee transportation system users, that may continue to occur with each successive special event at a particular venue location. As a result, stakeholders can develop and implement appropriate strategies (e.g., enforcement, etc.) and regulations to mitigate the identified impact(s) for future planned special events.

— Post-event debriefings represent a common and recommended stakeholder activity for all rural events.

a) Written comments should be obtained from temporary, borrowed staff used on the day-of-event if staff can not participate in a debriefing meeting.

b) A key aspect of a post-event debriefing for rural events involves preparing detailed meeting minutes that include the identification of key successes and lessons learned.

c) Considering the potential significant time between rural events, stakeholders must chronicle participant survey results and debriefing meetings so that those stakeholders charged with managing travel for future rural events can tap the wisdom of past participants.

— The occurrence of a major, recurring rural event warrants development of a post-event report. In turn, the report can serve as a working document to assist in advance planning for the next (year's) event.

— A post-event report for a recurring rural event should include an operational cost analysis to assist stakeholders in identifying potential cost-saving resource deployment strategies for the next event occurrence.

Programme Planning for Rural Events

Programme planning activities involve the development of policies, programmes, and initiatives that facilitate improved planning and management of travel for future planned special events. Programme planning for rural events include activities, as summarised in Table 1, on both a regional and local level.

Table 1. Programme Planning Activities for Rural Events

Product	Topic
Institutional frameworks	Development of a formal planned special event permit programme.
	Creation of a transportation operations task force for a recurring rural event or specific permanent venue.
	Development of a joint operations policy.
	Development of a mutual-aid agreement to facilitate resource sharing.
Policies and regulations	Traffic and parking restrictions.
	Public-private towing agreements.
	Public information safety campaign.
	High occupancy vehicle incentives.
Infrastructure deployment	Planned alternate route for diverting background traffic around a venue.
	Portable traffic management system.
	Express, charter or shuttle bus service.
	Telephone information systems.

Some distinguishing considerations of this event category during the programme planning phase include:

— The fixed location of planned special event venues (e.g., fairgrounds, amphitheaters, golf courses, and race tracks) in rural areas allow for the easy identification of stakeholder representatives involved in planning and day-of-event travel management for high-attendance special events at these venues. These representatives may collaborate year-round as an inter-jurisdictional, multi-discipline task force, working to:

a) strengthen interagency coordination for future special events,

b) identify needs relative to minimising community impacts and improving transportation system operations during venue events. The latter involves proposing new policies, regulations, and infrastructure deployments to support future event-specific traffic management plans and travel demand management initiatives.

— A planned special event permit programme proves particularly effective for rural events that, because of such characteristics as event attendance and event location, may

a) conflict with municipal or state guidelines and regulations and

b) impact transportation operations and the community.

— The programme specifies a permit process, coupled with supporting restrictions and requirements, that allow stakeholders to plan and assess all types of rural events within a common framework.

— Two or more stakeholders, representing multiple jurisdictions and/or disciplines, may establish a joint operations policy for managing travel for all planned special events in a region.

— Stakeholders may develop a mutual-aid agreement to facilitate resource sharing (e.g., personnel or equipment) and/or reimbursement for services in order to handle future planned special events.

— Because rural events usually occur infrequently and occasionally at temporary venues, an infrastructure needs assessment on the programme planning level should focus on equipment and technology applications transferable to managing all planned special events in a region and/or day-to-day transportation system operations.

— Funding represents a key public agency consideration for rural events in the programme planning phase.

a) Commercial events may involve event organisers and participants from outside the community hosting the event.

b) Prior to initiating event operations planning activities for a specific rural event, stakeholders should establish a funding mechanism for recovering costs incurred in providing services during the event operations planning phase and resources on the day-of-event.

c) Funding often represents a requirement of a comprehensive planned special event permit programme.

9

CRITICAL EVENT MANAGEMENT

Development of good practice in the management of critical events is essential to ensure that the best interests, rights, safety and welfare of children and young persons in out-of-home care are promoted. It is not possible to outline a definitive set of events or incidents that can be defined as critical events. It is more useful to give some identifying features of a critical event. It will be a matter for the principal officer or their delegate to make a judgement call based on the age, vulnerability and circumstances of the child or young person.

In determining whether an incident constitutes a critical event a good test is to ask the following questions:

— Has a child or young person in out-of-home care been seriously harmed or injured?

— Has a child or young person in out-of-home care been involved in an incident where they may have been seriously harmed?

— Could the event be subject to an official inquiry?

— Could the event be subject to community interest?

A critical event may be characterised by, but is not restricted to the following factors:

— It has a significant impact for a child or young person and possibly other persons involved.

— It is complex and may require additional supports for resolution and effective management.

— The nature of its seriousness necessitates an internal review of casework practice and management.

— It may be associated with or raise significant practice and/or systemic issues.

— It may have implications for service delivery.

— It may invoke intense media interest and public scrutiny.

— The associated stress may immobilise staff and/or carers and threaten placement continuity.

— It may be associated with breaches of the Act, the Regulations or accreditation requirements.

Critical events include (but are not limited to) the following circumstances:

— The death of a child or young person in out-of-home care.

— The death of a carer, parent, sibling, friend or caseworker with whom the child or young person has developed a relationship.

— A serious or life threatening condition for a child or young person resulting from abuse or neglect, non-accidental injury or unknown cause.

— Any fractures sustained by a child under six years.

— The advent of serious risk-taking behaviour in a child or young person, e.g. self-medication, self-mutilation, serious self-harm or suicide attempts.

— Any unexplained absence of a child or young person from an out-of-home care placement. For example, a runaway, a kidnapping or the failure of a parent to return a child following contact.

— The abuse of drugs or alcohol by a child or young person.

— Any acute psychiatric admission of a child or young person.

— Any allegation by a child or young person of sexual assault, by a carer or member of the carer's family, any resident or employee of residential care, staff member of a designated agency or any other person known to the carer's family.

— Any allegation by a child or young person of unlawful restraint by a carer or member of the carer's family, staff member of a designated agency or any other person known to the carer's family.

— Serious illness or incapacity of an authorised carer.

— Any serious threat of physical harm made to a child or young person, or members of the carer family or designated agency, e.g. a bomb threat or threats to assault or kill.

— Any allegation that a child or young person in out-of-home care may have committed a serious criminal offence.

— Any allegation that an authorised carer may have committed a serious criminal offence.

— The unauthorised use of behaviour management practices.

— The use of a prohibited behaviour management practice.

The death of a child or young person in out-of-home care is the most serious type of critical event. All designated agencies need to ensure that they have structured procedures and clear lines of responsibility to follow in the event of a death. When a child or young person dies the authorised carer is required at law to immediately notify the nearest police station and their designated agency.

The parents and/or family of the deceased child or young person have to be notified of the death where possible, in person, by the principal officer or their delegate. The death of a parent or an authorised carer is a critical event. Critical events such as these may require a placement review to determine whether the safety, welfare and well-being of a child or young person is being promoted.

Objectives of Critical Event Management Policy

A critical event management policy should always have as its paramount consideration the best interests, safety, welfare and well-being of children and young persons. It should aim to:

1. Reduce the incidence of critical event(s) in out-of-home care.
2. Ensure designated agency staff and authorised carers know and understand their responsibilities in relation to the reporting and management of critical events and incidents in out-of-home care.
3. Ensure designated agencies have structured procedures to follow and clear lines of responsibility, in the event of the death of a child or young person in out-of-home care.
4. Improve the quality of out-of-home care services for children and young persons and their families, by focusing the attention of out-of-home care service providers on understanding the circumstances of a critical event(s) and its implications for policy and/or practice changes within a particular agency or for the sector.

5. Meet a range of legislative requirements such as Occupational Health and Safety.

Development of a Framework

A useful approach when developing a critical event management policy is to focus separately on what are preventative measures and the strategies that can be used to manage a crisis in the immediate, short term and long term. A crucial component of critical event management is analysis and review. An organisation needs to use this type of information to determine the currency and appropriateness of its preventative and crisis management strategies. The following table provides guidance in terms of preventative measures as well as strategies that can be used in the immediate, short and long term management of a critical event:

Prevention of Critical Events

1. Comprehensive policy on critical event management that is clear and accessible to management, staff, carers and children and young persons. For example, a behaviour management policy that deals with the management of potentially dangerous behaviour and emergency procedures in case of an accident.
2. Regular reviews of policy and procedure documents and of the case plans of children and young persons in out-of-home care.
3. Clear lines of verbal and written communication and documentation between management, staff and carers.
4. A complaints monitoring system.
5. A method of collecting and evaluating stakeholder feedback.
6. Regular staff and carer training on critical event management. Staff and authorised carers need to be

aware of their responsibilities in relation to critical event management and reporting. Regard should be had to the Children's Guardian's guidelines on the exercise of care responsibility and religious instruction by authorised carers and guidelines for designated agencies for developing a behaviour management policy.

7. Early identification and reporting of critical events can prevent their escalation.
8. Comprehensive intake and assessment procedures assist in collecting necessary information regarding a child, including medical history, care and family history, so that any risks or problems can be identified and planned for.
9. Appropriate matching of children and young persons and carers that takes into account the needs of the child or young person and the extent to which these are able to be met by the carer.
10. Good knowledge and use of community resources and liaison with other service providers, such as youth services and health centres, which can assist in preventing critical events.
11. Knowledge about and access to legal advice through the Youth Hotline or Law Access NSW can help improve situations.
12. Knowledge of the rights of children and young persons in out-of-home care.

Crisis and Short Term Management

1. Ensure that immediate action is taken to secure the safety, both physical and emotional, of any child or young person involved in or affected by a critical event.

2. Ensure that any child or young person involved in or affected by a critical event is provided with support, assistance and appropriate counselling.
3. As may be appropriate, the provision of assistance and support to the carer(s) and their family as a consequence of the critical event.
4. As may be appropriate, the provision of assistance and support to the child or young person's parents and their family as a consequence of the critical event.
6. Early investigation, assessment and monitoring of a critical event to reduce the likelihood of further harm to children and young persons.
7. Early risk assessment in relation to any child or young person affected by a critical event to determine how to best ensure their continued care and protection and determine if there is any need for a change of placement.
8. Ensure the appropriate people and authorities are informed in a timely manner of the circumstances of any child or young person in out-of-home care, who may be involved in or affected by a critical event.
9. To ensure parents and any significant others are advised about any critical event that involves their child or young person whilst in out-of-home care.
10. A written record is made in relation to any critical event at the time or as soon as possible after the event. This record should be signed and dated by the person who witnessed and/or took the first details about the critical event and the principal officer or their delegate.

Long Term Critical Event Management

1. Senior management should conduct an internal investigation of the circumstances that led to the critical event and review the procedures that were in

place at the time to deal with the matter. They should ensure that any service improvements suggested by the review are introduced.

2. Review the overall policies and procedures of the agency with respect to identifying and addressing any inadequacies or breaches.
3. Review the case plan of the child and young person and if appropriate, a specific review of the behaviour management plans for that child.
4. A review of staff training and supervision.
5. A review of disciplinary procedures if the critical event involved misconduct by a staff member.

Indigenous Children and Young Persons

When formulating policy in relation to Indigenous children and young persons and the management of critical events in an Indigenous context, designated agencies should ensure that their policy is relevant to the region where their service is located. If the child or young person does not come from the region where the service is located a different approach may be more appropriate. To address such cases, the designated agency should develop broad policy in consultation with key Indigenous stakeholders. When an agency is unsure about the correct process of incorporating management of a critical event in an Indigenous community into policy, it is recommended that the agency follow a consultative process with Aboriginal organisations and/or Government, to seek advice.

Aboriginal organisations may be able to provide links with appropriate community members who may be able to advise the designated agency on the most appropriate way to handle the critical event. Designated agencies need to assess critical events on a case-by-case basis and take a common sense approach. Sensitivity needs to be considered in the management of a critical event. For example, as with non-Indigenous cases, it may not be appropriate to consult with the family and/or the community if hypothetically the critical event is around abuse and it has occurred within the family and/or community.

When a designated agency formulates policy around the management of critical events for Indigenous children and young persons in out-of-home care they could consider the following:

— The region where their service is located in assessing the type of policy which would be appropriate for a child and/or young person who is from the local community. For example, are there family nearby who need to be informed and/or consulted and if so, how will the agency undertake this process?

— How their service will manage a critical event where the child and/or young person is not from the community where their service is located and what steps will be taken to manage the event effectively? For example, the agency may need to contact an Aboriginal agency operating in the community where the child or young person comes from to inform family members and/or consult with family and/or the community if appropriate.

— How will the agency manage grief and loss issues across the community should they arise?

Culturally and Linguistically Diverse (CALD) Children and Young Persons

Designated agencies which arrange care for children and young persons from culturally and linguistically diverse (CALD) backgrounds should formulate policy which takes into consideration the child and/or young person's cultural background. Some of the issues an agency should consider when developing policy around critical events involving children and young persons from CALD backgrounds include:

- Religion of the child and/or young person and how their religious needs can be met should there be a critical incident;
- Diversity of burial practices in different cultures;
- Location of relatives, if overseas;
- Language of the child and/or young person and their family and/or community and whether an interpreter is required if a critical event occurs;
- Background of the child or young person, i.e. whether the child or young person is a recent migrant and/or refugee, and possible steps to overcome this complexity, such as involving another agency that specialises in migrant and refugee issues; and
- How the child and/or young person will be involved in decision making.

10

Lighting of Events

Event lighting is a cross between theatre, concert, residential, and decorative lighting, each of which is a separate discipline and has had volumes written about it. There is no specific event lighting discipline, and the experts in the field have created their own competency.

The lighting designer is the man who plans the lighting design, does the light plot, and provides the preliminary light cues. The lighting director is the on-site lighting expert who supervises the installation, runs the crew, makes on-site adjustments to the plot, and programmes the final cues. In theatre this is usually the same person, but in touring shows and in most audiovisual and many production companies and probably at your next event, the lighting director and the lighting designer may be different professionals. A production company is one that supplies the lights and sound for a show or event. A large production company may have several productions running concurrently but only one lighting designer.

The lighting design is both the original aesthetic phase and the functionally necessary phase of lighting. This is where the aesthetic decisions that create the final mood and focus are made and where the inventory that will be required to achieve these effects is compiled. The designer creates the light plot, which is the plan that shows where each instrument is hung, what colour or colours it will have in it, and how it will be circuited, or patched. This plan is drawn as a reflected ceiling, which is essentially a floor plan with the light rigging and instruments overlaid on it. There also will be a sectional view illustrating a cross section of the room and the angle at which the light will be illuminating the stage, decor, and performers.

Light plots can be drafted by hand, but most designers work in a Computer Aided Design and Drafting (CADD) format. It is convenient but not essential that the event designer be able to read a light plot, but he or she should at least understand the principles of scale drawing and representative symbols, such as those explained in the key in this drawing. Frequently an event designer or decorator is hired after the production company is in place or has to hire a production company in another town. In these cases, it is valuable to have an event professional who is knowledgeable about lighting and other aspects of production such as sound and staging to call on to serve as the production manager.

The lighting designer needs to be on the same wavelength as the event designer. The theme is very important to the lighting designer. Event lighting involves a lot of compromises. One cannot always put instruments where he/she want to, especially in tents. Designing in advance, pre-planning, and coordinating execution with all the other elements are crucial. The designer needs to be choosy about which instruments to use. The power source can be a challenge. Working with generators will be more grateful. Coordinate all the technical people for dark time, sound checks, focus, and power so that they all get what they need when they need it-the production time line is so important.

Lighting for Small Events

Lighting is as important for small events as it is for large ones. The ambience, or atmosphere, is created by and can be destroyed by the lighting. Think of being at a dance with dim, romantic lighting and what happens when it is over and the lights are turned on full. Many times lighting a small event is simply a matter of dimming the existing lights. However, this dims all the lights, including those on the flowers, food, and guest tables, and does not add any enhancements to the decor. With some readily available equipment it is possible to add atmosphere by washing the walls with colour, accent the decor with spotlights, or pin-spot the centerpieces.

Dimmer control over existing lights either exists or it does not. If it does not, consider adding dimmers to the existing circuitry. However, lights also can be dimmed by unscrewing selected lightbulbs or replacing them with lower-watt bulbs. Colour can be added either by exchanging the existing lamps (lightbulbs) for coloured lamps or by putting gel (heat-resistant plastic film colour media) over them. Existing light fixtures can be gelled by securing colour media in front of the lamp, taping or pinning it to the trim, fixture, or ceiling. Plan this in advance and try it in the darkened room to make sure it works and does what you want it to do.

Backlight-light coming from an instrument behind rather than in front of fabric-is especially effective and can be done in colours. Uplight on foliage plants, trees, and many other decorations can be dramatic, but do not uplight people. Adding light to draw attention to a specific item or area or removing or dimming existing lighting around that item is called accent lighting. Accent lighting also can involve adding colour. This can entail lighting (accenting) floral arrangements or decor, lighting a musical combo, or lighting the area where the best man will make a toast. Extension sockets, goosenecks or clip-on lights with spots, and floodlights work for accent lighting. Colour can be created by using coloured lamps or by putting gel over them.

The lamps commonly used with these fixtures include PAR lamps and R-type lamps, which come in various sizes and wattages, as do MR-16 lamps. Clear PAR 38 lamps come in spot and flood. They are available in colours, including several shades of pink and blue and a cool blue-white colour, usually only in 100 watts. These different lamps come from different manufacturers, and finding a useful blend of colours is a matter of trial and error. If you are accenting with swivel extension sockets or goosenecks in existing ceiling lights, remember that they will be dimmed when the lights are lowered. Use higher-wattage lights in this case so that they will be brighter than the surrounding dim light.

Lighting for Stage Events

Any event that has a live stage production to be lighted, even if it is only a dance band or a speaker, needs to have the required lighting (and sound) integrated into the event design and decor. If it is not, the band equipment will not fit or will hide the pretty stuff or add an unplanned technical look. A best practice for the professional event designer and decorator is to find out what is going to be on the stage for entertainment or production before the stage is designed or the decor is planned.

Many bands and all name entertainment acts include a rider or technical rider as part of the contract. This document legally obligates the signer to provide very specific sound, light, and other production equipment for the performance.

Most productions today require a front and a rear truss with PAR cans and a number of intelligent lights. In addition, there may be several lekos for "specials" and for projecting gobos on the stage, walls, or dance floor and one or two follow spots. All operators will have to be connected via a Clear Com or another communications setup to the lighting director (LD), the stage manager, or whoever is the cue caller.

Typical lighting for a show band includes a three-colour wash from a front truss along with several specials to light the stars or highlight the main performance area, a rear truss in several colours, a follow spot, and several intelligent lights. The colour wash typically is supplied by 1-kilowatt PAR cans or the equivalent; lekos are used for specials and gobo projections. The follow spot will be set up at the rear of the room on a tower to raise it and the operator above the crowd.

Lighting for Large Events

Large events typically include a stage show plus additional general lighting and/or effect lighting. General lighting in large events can require a lot of electricity and a lot of rigging to hang it from many different positions. The general rules for lighting events, given in Table 1, apply for large events as well as small ones. Power requirements can be reduced through the careful selection of lighting instruments. Uplighting the perimeter walls or the decor can alleviate the need for some rigging but puts power cable on the floor, where it must be dealt with at doorways.

General lighting washes can be done with PAR cans with colour changers, which can scroll through selected colours by means of remote programming. Projected gobos in what are called breakup patterns (small irregular patches of light) provide reduced light with a texture rather than just flooding an area with light.

Lighting for Tented events

Tented events pose special problems for the lighting designer because there are extremely limited hanging positions. Lighting in tents must be either ground-supported or supported from the tent poles. Many event designers and decorators have devised special tent pole clamps that support rigging for lighting from the center poles or quarter poles. Large lighting rigs are frequently supported by vertical truss supports that are secured to the tent poles.

Some tents are constructed of blackout fabric, which, although white, is opaque and blocks sunlight, requiring that lighting be supplied at all times. Other tents are made of traditional fabric, which allows light in. These tents depend on the weather for ambient light levels, and general lighting may or may not be needed. Sidewalls can be used or left off; they can be clear or have windows sewn into them. These options will affect the amount of lighting needed.

Tents do not have power sources and require either running power to a disconnect from an existing breaker box or transformer on the property or using a portable silenced generator. Tents are temporary structures that leak in heavy rain storms and move in heavy, gusty winds. Professional tent rental companies that service the special event industry may supply some form of general lighting for use in their tents. This can consist of track lights that are secured vertically to the tent poles or PAR cans that are clamped to the perimeter poles and shine up to reflect off the white tent canvas top. Most of these companies have in-line dimmers available. Beyond this minimal lighting, a professional lighting designer with experience in tented events should be employed for aesthetic, functional, and risk management reasons.

Good lighting Techniques

Good lighting designers must be competent in three areas.

— They must be technically competent with the equipment.

— They must be operationally competent, organised, and capable of handling resources and risk management.

— They need to understand the aesthetic principles of good lighting design.

Some general rules for lighting events effectively are given in Table 1.

Table 1. General rules for lighting events

General rules for lighting events
— Warm white or light pink is a flattering colour for people.
— Blue is romantic but not flattering.
— Dim is romantic but hard to eat or talk by.
— Backlighting is always romantic.
— A blend of pink and blue generally works well for events.
— Too much light is as bad as too little.
— Only white light should be used on food or flowers.
— White is an excellent accent colour when surrounded by coloured light.
— Spots draw attention.
— Green light makes greenery look artificial.
— Green light makes people look dead.
— When you are lighting flowers or other decor, sit in the chair or stand where the guests will be standing and make sure the light will not be in their eyes.
— Everything you do with lighting, every decision you make, should have a reason or it will look inappropriate or out of place.

Unfortunately, many have considerably more training in the technical and operational aspects of lighting than in the aesthetic principles. It is important that the event designer know what lights can do and be able to communicate clearly what he or she wants to the lighting designer.

Selection of Colours

White light is a combination of all other colours of light. Blending combinations of primary red, primary blue, and primary green light in different proportions creates all the colours in the visible light spectrum. Black is the absence of light. Light is invisible and is revealed when it falls on an object that is being viewed. These basic concepts can be confusing because we are more used to talking about colour as paints or pigments. If you mix many different colours of light together, you get white light. As a result of the impurities in pigment, if you mix many colours of paint together, you get gray or brown, colours that cannot be achieved in light.

Colour is achieved either by using coloured lamps (light bulbs) or by putting colour filters, called gels, in front of the instrument (light fixture). Reflected light also will pick up the colour of whatever it bounces off. Some basic practical results of these principles of colour that the event designer will discover include the following:

— Bright colours are not achieved by putting a lot of colours together but by keeping them separated. A bright, multicoloured look is achieved by lighting in different colours that do not overlap. When they overlap, they blend and become white.

— Pure white light looks unnatural to the spectator or audience because most natural and artificial light is a combination of white light and the reflected light from the surfaces from which it bounces.

— "Natural" light on stage generally is achieved by using a warm colour (light pink or light amber) on one side, a cool colour (light blue) on the other, and a neutral colour (light lavender) from the front to create a blended white light. These colours should be spectrum-balanced to achieve a white when mixed together.

— Lighting on a brightly coloured floor will reflect that colour on the decor, the scenery, and the people who walk on it.

— Because light tends to blend to white in nature, any saturated colour will seem unnatural and/or have a dramatic effect. Some examples are "moonlight" blue, which has a dramatic romantic effect; red "flames," which have a dramatic "hot" impact; and green light, which looks unnatural, especially on greenery and people.

— Because light is invisible and a mirror reflects light, you cannot "light" a mirror. In the case of mirrors or reflective glass, such as windows at night, the way to light them is to light what will be reflected in them.

Angle of Incidence

The angle of incidence is the angle at which light beams strike the object being lighted. The optimal natural lighting would have the cool and warm lights striking the object at 45 degrees off center and the neutral light dead center, all mounted above the object or person being lighted at a 45-degree angle from vertical. The addition of a backlight puts an attractive halo around the speaker or performer. The three-point system starts with a primary light source at 45 degrees, called the key light, and adds fill light at a lower angle and from the opposite side to light the environment and fill in the shadows; then backlight is added. Other lighting practices that are used today were developed for rock concerts.

The basic light plot is typically a three-colour wash so that colours can be alternated to match the music or blended to achieve different stage pictures and a reasonably attractive and natural-looking front light. This typically is achieved by circuiting and colouring every third PAR can separately and using them to flood the stage evenly in one of the three colours selected or in a blend of those colours. Other angles of interest to the event designer include the following:

— Sidelight emphasises contours and profiles of scenery and people and enhances movement.

— Very steep angles or overhead lights throw dramatic shadows. These dramatic angles are not always flattering and most often are used as backlight. Steep sidelight can be very effective at creating sunrise and sunset atmospheres.

— Uplight looks very weird and unflattering on people and has been used for horror effects for years, but it also can be used to light the ceiling to match the stage.

— Lighting for backdrops and curtains requires special mention. A front wash or a wash from both sides equally washes out wrinkles. Uplight, sidelight, or downlight will emphasise the wrinkles and can ruin an otherwise brilliant backdrop. However, for the same reasons, this oblique lighting looks good on a pleated, swagged, or contour curtain, emphasising the sewn-in depth and texture.

Range of Light Levels

Everybody has to deal with light levels at events, if only by adjusting the house lights. Dimming is the one area of lighting in which people know almost everything they need to know from experience. The human eye and brain are amazingly adaptable and adjust in just a few minutes to be comfortable in a broad range of light levels. There are just a few things an event manager needs to be aware of. If you want to bring attendees' focus to a specific area, using light to give a logo, speaker, or product prominence, you can raise the level of light in that area or on that object or you can lower the level of light around it. The two most common light level problems are not having enough light in work situations and having too much light in party situations.

Speakers are easier to hear if they are well lighted. This is the case because we "hear" a certain amount with our eyes by reading body language and seeing the way lips form words. Also, the speaker will have our attention if he or she is the brightest object in the room. Celebrations and social gatherings generally require a low level of ambient light, which creates a relaxing ambience. How low a level depends on the goal of the gathering. A bride needs to be seen when she arrives at the reception, and the family and friends need enough light to recognise one another easily. As dinner is served, the light level can go down a bit more but should remain high enough that people can see to enjoy the meal. Late in the evening the festivities will be enhanced by still a lower level for dancing. Corporate celebrations are very similar, except for sales and marketing events, or networking events, where the light levels should remain higher longer. Also, participant demographics affect the amount of light for an event. Older people need more light to see by, and younger crowds like it dark.

Pin-spotting flower arrangements on guest tables has become very popular. One or more extremely narrow beam instruments are used to illuminate individual centerpieces from overhead. Expensive flowers do not have to become invisible when the light level is lowered; instead, they seem to glow from within. Another benefit of pin-spotting arrangements is that the pin spots frequently throw a small area of ambient light onto the table, creating lowlevel party ambience throughout the room while giving the guests enough light to see the food and one another.

When using pin spots or other accent lighting that is plugged into the same sockets as the general lighting for the room, remember that those lights will be dimmed when the rest of the lights are dimmed. To work around this, unplug or unscrew the balance of the lights in the dimmable circuit or use brighter lights in the accent lights than in the rest of the fixtures. Tents, especially open tents or tents with clear sidewall, pose another challenge at sunset. The human eye can be fooled as the sun goes down, and people perceive the twilight as darkness. It is desirable to raise the light level at that time. When darkness is achieved, it can be lowered to a level appropriate for the activity or goal of the evening.

Computer-controlled Lighting

Computer-controlled moving iights are referred to generically as intelligent lighting, robotic lights, or moving lights. These lights vary in their capabilities, depending on the manufacturer and the model, but they all feature a computer programmed to control a moving light beam that changes colour and may also change shape or be used to project patterns called gobos. To show the moving beams, it is standard practice to haze the room with a nontoxic mineral oil fog from a fogger or hazer.

The Vari-Lite Company of Dallas, Texas, developed the first intelligent lights, patenting them in 1983. They featured moving beams of light and dichroic lens colour changing, which allowed almost instantaneous colour changes with up to 60 colours. They were first used in rock concerts and tours. They brought a new dimension to lighting, and many other companies developed different intelligent lighting instruments.

With the explosion of intelligent lighting, it did not take people long to get tired of moving lights. The challenge for the event designer is to use intelligent lighting intelligently. A bank of bright white moving lights can move together from upstage to downstage and then break into individual moving lights rotating around the stage and room in changing colours and patterns. This is a very effective light cue the first time. If it is used over and over, it becomes tiresome, then annoying. Effects add impact to an event when they are unexpected. Constantly or too frequently moving lights lose their effect.

Lighting Instruments

Events in small ballrooms, country clubs, and residences require fewer and smaller lighting instruments and equipment. Lower ceilings mean a shorter throw (the distance between the light fixture and the object being lighted). Bulky and expensive theatrical lighting equipment may be inappropriate when residential or industrial equipment can be used or modified to provide lighting for small venues.

Different theatrical lighting instruments put out light with a different character because of the differences in lenses, reflectors, and light sources. The white light in the beam varies widely depending on the light source. These details are beyond the need to know of an event designer, but some degree of understanding and familiarity is required.

In the relatively near future, the entire incandescent technology behind the lightbulb may be replaced by LED (light-emitting diode) technology. Currently the cutting-edge technological developments are in lighting control, which is 90 percent computer-controlled in theatre and special event applications.

The biggest trend in lighting right now is in the control systems, as the manufacturers are refining WYSIWYG, a software acronym that stands for 'what you see is what you get'. In functional terms, this means that there are two monitor screens in the studio. One shows the three-dimensional image of the actual stage set to be lighted, and the other shows the lighting rig. The designer can then write the cues for the show in advance and see them represented on the replica stage, including light beams in colours. This is potentially a tremendous saving in time.

Risk in lighting Events

Every aspect of special events requires careful attention to risk management, and in no other specialty is that as apparent as it is in lighting, where we routinely hang tons of equipment over the heads of guests and attendees. There is also an electrical hazard, as we are dealing with temporary electrical cables and some extremely high-amperage (amp) loads. In addition to these obvious factors, there is concern about the heat generated by lighting equipment, which is sufficiently high to set fire to combustible material, and the trip hazard of power cables.

Rigging and electrical hazards are best managed by hiring only trained professionals, licensed and certified where applicable. It is a good practice to use the in-house show electrician and riggers, and many venues require it. The heat generated from lighting instruments can be a hidden threat as the instruments are often high in the air or concealed from view for aesthetic reasons. They represent concealed fire hazards.

Using only flame-retardant material does not mean that one should relax one's vigilance. The heat from lighting instruments can damage valuable drops or curtains even if flames do not break out. Special care is also required around table linens or existing drapery, as the flameretardant quality of these materials is unknown and is likely to be insufficient to protect against fire.

Another area of concern is lighting in or around trees and foliage, especially cut winter holiday trees and foliage. Pine, fir, and balsam trees and garland must be flame-retardant-treated, as they are extremely flammable. One of the biggest nightmares of many lighting designers is the mass of cable and how to conceal it. Safety is a huge part of lighting events, including rigging safety and cable on the floor safety.

Cables should be run overhead whenever possible, and when they are on the floor, small bundles of cables can be taped down with high-visibility tape and, if possible, taped flat to the floor and covered with a piece of carpet that is taped to the floor to create a ramp. For large cables and large bunches of cables, commercial cable ramps are available that provide a visible ramp for people and protection to the cables in vehicular situations, such as running cables across a driveway.

11

Traffic Management for Special Events

During the advance planning process, countless meetings were attended, numerous hours were spent developing and reworking the traffic management plan, and every contingency was considered. Now, the day is here and it is time to implement and operate the plan. Not only do the requirements of the traffic management plan have to be considered, but also it is essential to monitor what can be a very fluid situation to see how the plan is working and then determine what needs to be adjusted based on real-time traffic conditions.

Always expect the unexpected and be ready to handle that unplanned situation. Assess the adequacy of the established communications structure and determine if it is possible to deploy what is needed in a timely manner. Following are the important day-of-event activities.

- Implement a management process for the traffic management team.
- Designate a multi-agency command post.
- Conduct a traffic management plan evaluation(s) during the day-of-event.
- Establish protocol for traffic management team officials to consider and implement changes to the traffic

management plan to accommodate real-time traffic conditions.

— Establish interagency communication protocol.
— Review communication equipment compatibility.
— Use the media to communicate with event patrons and other transportation users.
— Perform traffic monitoring on the day-of-event.

Traffic Management Team

The traffic management team includes not only many of those stakeholders that have been involved during the event operations planning phase, but all those who may be involved for the first time on the day of the event. This includes other event support stakeholders, other stakeholder representatives, and volunteer personnel. Following are the typical stakeholders involved in day-of-event activities.

— Traffic operations agency
— Transit agency
— Law enforcement
— Public safety
— Event organiser
— Transportation consultants
— Traffic control contractors
— Emergency management agency

A planned special event represents a source of non-recurring congestion where, similar to a traffic incident, stakeholders must adopt a formal management process to ensure successful traffic management plan deployment and minimal impact to transportation system users. The Incident Command System can be used to handle traffic management during planned special events. The ICS organises and coordinates multi-agency response to an incident by establishing responsibilities and lines of authority. An Incident Commander has overall responsibility for managing the planned special event.

Depending upon the size of the event a number of individuals will report to the Incident Commander. A key to the ICS is that the reporting relationships be kept to a manageable size. If the number of people reporting to a single individual grows too large, another layer of command should be added. Unified Command represents an ICS management process that functions to coordinate inter-jurisdictional and multi-disciplinary stakeholders comprising the traffic management team without sacrificing agency authority, responsibility, or accountability.

The Unified Command hierarchy includes the Incident Commander serving to coordinate and manage the activities performed by stakeholders classified under the following organisational elements: branches, groups, and units. A branch agency manages a specific operational function. For example, a law enforcement agency is responsible for traffic control and pedestrian accommodation. Group agencies manage and execute specific functional activities. Units execute specific functional activities. For instance, a private towing company is responsible for removing illegally parked or disabled vehicles.

Per Unified Command protocol, if an unexpected event happens during the planned special event, a transfer of command may occur. The decision to effect a transfer of command depends on the qualifications and experience of all on-site branch agency supervisors relative to that of the acting Incident Commander. For example, if a severe weather event took place during a planned special event, an emergency management agency official may assume the role of Incident Commander.

An advantage of using the ICS during a planned special event is that it clarifies how decisions are made if the traffic management plan requires adjustment. Unexpected events may necessitate adjusting the plan to meet changing circumstances. In this instance, there may not be the luxury of meeting with all stakeholders to develop a consensus on how to modify the plan. The Incident Commander should have the authority to make those adjustments that are needed.

Team Management

Typically for a planned special event, a representative of a law enforcement agency will take on the role of Incident Commander. Representatives of various agencies will, in turn, report to the Incident Commander. Among those working under the Incident Commander will be one or more transportation representatives. A lead person should be identified for each agency responsible for part of the traffic management plan. Among those who may be a part of the transportation team are representatives from the state department of transportation, local traffic agencies, toll agencies and transit agencies. Depending upon what is worked out in the event operations planning phase, all of these individuals may be represented by a single Incident Commander (e.g., transportation commander) or by individuals representing each of their respective agencies.

Role of Command Post

The ICS will most likely be used in a multi-agency command post. In some instances, a permanent TMC may serve as the primary command post. The advantage of using the TMC is that many of the communications resources and other needed tools are already in place. If the TMC is used, the ICS should still be employed if multiple agencies comprise the traffic management team. This operation would likely differ from typical activities in the TMC, given the presence of multiple outside agency representatives.

In the event operations planning phase, the ICS would be used to identify who is the Incident Commander at the TMC and how activities are coordinated within the TMC during the event. Advantages of a single command post include: (1) key agencies are represented in a single location and (2) communications among agencies are simplified. An advantage of secondary command posts is that event management can be more easily switched if a problem develops at the primary command post.

Resource Planning

The plan developed for the resources needed for the event represent the collected best opinion on what is needed. Resource planning involves the following two parts: (1) determining the scope and amount of resources that will be used on the day-of-event and (2) identifying resources in advance in case the traffic management team needs more resources than planned to implement the traffic management plan. The most important resource that stakeholders must plan for involve personnel resources. Planning considerations include:

— What type and quantity of skilled personnel are needed?

— Where should personnel be deployed?

— What responsibilities will individual personnel have?

Most day of event field personnel will work in areas different from their normal, day-to-day work location. Relief for personnel may be more difficult to obtain because of agency constraints, and relief assignment should be part of personnel planning. Field personnel may require frequent breaks in difficult weather conditions, and traffic management team officials may have to substitute back-up staff if planned relief is not available. The operation of planned special events on the day-of-event includes three phases: ingress, the event itself, and egress.

Resources need to be available for all three phases with emphasis on ingress and egress. The traffic management team will likely need fewer personnel for traffic management during the event, and part of the planning should include what level of staffing is needed during this period. Depending on the length of the event, a second shift may report to handle egress. If a first (ingress) and second (egress) shift exists, traffic management team officials can stagger work times (e.g., first shift individual reporting later and leaving later or second shift individual reporting early and leaving early) to maintain sufficient personnel on-site during the event. Another consideration concerns how quickly staff and other resources can be deployed incase the event ends sooner than expected, thus causing early departures.

Traffic Management

While the traffic management plan and supporting implementation plan notes how stakeholders expect to manage traffic, the actual management of traffic on the day-of-event may differ from what the plan calls for. Traffic incidents, changing weather conditions, and other unexpected events can all cause the traffic management plan to be modestly modified or completely changed. After safety, successfully managing traffic represents the reason why stakeholders developed the traffic management plan in the first place and that goal must remain paramount.

As part of the traffic management plan, various scenarios can be addressed from best case to worst case, together with likely variations. Having different scenarios and response plans specified in the traffic management plan will help managers more quickly respond to changes. Again, not every variation can be noted, but experienced staff can modify what the traffic management plan calls for. When done well, managing traffic is done on a proactive basis, anticipating what will happen next and reacting before problems cascade.

Like an orchestra conductor, the traffic managers are calling on different elements to play as the event proceeds. A traffic queue in one area will require adjustments to signal timing on primary and alternate routes. Traffic incidents not only require response to the site of the incident but the activation of appropriate messages on roadside traveller information devices. As a general rule, drivers tend to be more understanding about a congestion delay if they are informed of what is taking place and are assured steps are being taken to mitigate the problem.

To properly manage traffic, the managers need timely and accurate information. Staff in the field must understand the importance of the information they provide, and staff at the command centre must help the managers understand the information coming in, such as pointing out what is most important. Too much information without some interpretation is almost as worthless as too little information. Other staff should be on hand to assist with other activities taking place in the command centre. This includes handling VIPs, disseminating information to the media, and addressing routine items such as equipment problems.

Evaluation activities

Although many hours have been spent creating the traffic management plan, the plan should remain flexible with the ability to modify and enhance it with necessary changes based on real-time traffic conditions. Updates can continue through the course of the planned special event, accounting for new situations and unexpected events. Evaluation of the plan is an ongoing activity during the event, and participants should contribute their insights as they witness the event unfolding. The traffic management team must be open to modifications of what had been agreed to during the event operations planning and implementation activities phases. Traffic management plan evaluation activities on the day-of-event are described below.

— Establish briefing schedule and location (e.g., command post).

— Identify ranking representative of each stakeholder agency participating in briefings.

— Conduct day-of-event briefing.

  a) Situation status

  b) Objectives and priorities

  c) Current organisation

  d) Personnel and equipment resource assignments

  e) Communications

  f) Concerns and related issues

  g) Recommended changes

— Achieve consensus on recommended changes.

There are several different ways to accomplish this evaluation and revision process:

— Some modifications will be minor in nature and will not require significant discussion. For example, moving a traffic post may be a simple change that improves the flow of traffic. The Incident Commander may have authority to make such a change.

— A more significant change, such as the route of buses to the venue site, involves a greater number of agencies and individuals. These changes need to be discussed before being implemented to make certain everyone affected is aware of the change so that any concerns with the proposed change are addressed and overcome.

— If the suggested change is urgent, a quick discussion among the agencies involved may suffice.

— If it is not urgent, the modification can be discussed during a regularly scheduled meeting of the stakeholder representatives.

How and if these meetings are scheduled can vary depending upon the dynamics of the planned special event:

— If the event is small in scale and only a few agencies are involved, there may be no need for scheduled meetings. Revisions can be easily discussed among participants at the command post.

— On the other hand, large events involving many stakeholders would require meetings to discuss: (1) what has taken place, (2) what lies ahead, and (3) what changes are recommended.

If scheduled meetings are planned, the next question is when to hold these meetings:

— If the event stretches over several days with a clear end time each day, it is logical to conduct a meeting at the end of each day's activities. At this point, the participants will not be distracted by managing the event, and they will have the benefit of their experience that day to decide what should be revised.

— If the event is longer, perhaps even running around-the-clock, regular meetings can be scheduled during expected lulls in activity. These meetings may be specifically scheduled in anticipation of key activities, such as the egress of event patrons.

— For events where a shift change is needed in the command centre, a meeting of the crew, or crew supervisor, going off-duty may be helpful so they can recommend changes to those relieving them.

Many of the same procedures used during the creation of the plan can be used to make revisions during the event. Those involved discuss the changes, call for input from those directly affected, and agree on what will be done. It is important that any changes be communicated to all involved. Major problems can develop if one group is operating under old assumptions. In many cases, having a computer and printer available will make updates easier to share.

If the plan is in a notebook or manual form, the revised section can just take the place of the old section. Participants should note on the revised plan that it represents an update and when that revision was made. This makes it easier to track changes and make certain everyone is operating with the same information.

Communication Structure

In most areas of the country, interoperable communications, in which all agencies are able to communicate on a common radio frequency, is not yet a reality. That being the case, it is necessary for a communication structure and protocol to be established. Primary considerations of communication structure are:

— What radio channels or frequencies will be used.

— Who will use these channels.

— Will a common lexicon be used for communications.

Whatever frequency is used, it is important that all those who must use it be able to access the channel and that coverage include all areas where operations will take place. In some cases, operating on a common frequency may require the distribution of radios to some of the stakeholders. In some instances, agencies have used cellular phones with a push-to-talk feature to provide a common channel during an event. Some agencies may already have these handsets and use them for day-to-day operations. One or more special talk channels can be established for use during the planned special event to allow only traffic management team members to be on the air.

Advantage

— Most of the infrastructure is provided by a private company.
— Coverage can be achieved over a wider area than some individual agencies enjoy.
— Agencies' normal channels are freed for regular operations.
— Other frequencies are not jammed with transmissions related to the planned special event.

Another important part of the protocol involves using common language on a multi-agency frequency. Many agencies use verbal shorthand in the form of codes when transmitting. These codes work well when used by those who know them, but when other stakeholders are involved, the codes can be a source of confusion and miscommunication. An increasing number of agencies are now using clear language protocols on their radio frequencies, and these standards should be followed if multiple agencies have to communicate with one another. Clear language simply says that commonly understood words and phrases are used instead of codes.

Interagency communication

Since multiple stakeholders are involved, it is critical that they be able to communicate with one another on the day-of-event:

— The most basic, and least desirable, form of interagency communication involves messages being relayed indirectly from one agency to another. An example could include a police officer in the field wishing to coordinate a road closure with the DOT. The officer radios the information to a dispatcher who, in turn, calls the dispatcher at the DOT. The DOT dispatcher then radios the crew in the field. Coordination might take several messages being sent back and forth through this chain. This form of communication delays the sharing of information and is subject to miscommunication.

— Operating on a common channel with clear language greatly improves interagency communication. Depending upon the size of the planned special event, more than one channel may be used. For example, one channel could be deemed as the primary channel, which is used by all participants for the sharing of critical information. Another channel may be dedicated to transportation concerns.

To minimise confusion and extraneous information being shared among agencies, the question of who will use which frequencies should be decided during the planning process. Stakeholders should understand:

a) how they can reach other traffic management team members during the event,

b) which channels they will be found on, and

c) what information should be shared.

Since many of the stakeholders comprising the traffic management team may not be accustomed to interagency coordination, they should understand the importance of sharing information with their interagency partners.

Information not shared with others who are affected could lead to difficulties managing traffic and cause mistrust among participating stakeholders.

The participating agencies may normally operate on a wide variety of systems. VHF, UHF, and 800 MHz trunked systems are among those in common use, and agencies cannot normally communicate from one system to another. Before the right equipment can be identified, it is important for the stakeholders to understand what they want the communications system to do. Is it simply a means to share information, or does real-time coordination have to take place? Who has to operate on the channel? Where will they be located? Once these questions are answered, it becomes possible to identify the appropriate equipment to use for the event. There are several levels of communication. These are:

— Within the venue

— Between individual stakeholders

— Between field staff and command post

— Between command post and TMCs

Another level of communication would be between the command post and the TMCs. Here it may be more difficult to identify the best equipment to use. The TMCs may be geographically distant from each other and the command post. Because the centers are inside buildings, and often on lower floors, radios without an external antenna may not be able to reach all the participating stakeholders. In order to depend upon these communication channels, it is important that they be tested before the event.

If no radio communication is practical, a hardwire connection may be needed. In some TMCs and command centers, phone jacks are installed to allow dedicated phones to be deployed for events. A trunked radio system provides what is needed for interagency communication during a planned special event. Other agencies, which also operate on a trunked system, may be able to modify their units to operate on a common frequency. A trunked system also allows a dedicated channel to be set aside for the event. Those agencies without the proper equipment can be loaned radios, which allow them to operate on the common channel.

Role of Media

The media is an important part of the planned special event. If the event involves a lot of people, it also is a news story and the media will want to cover it like any other story. The media can also be an important part of traffic management plan implementation. Before the event media is used as

— Identify preferred routes.

— Identify approved parking areas.

— Identify transit alternatives.

— Identify locations where event patrons can obtain travel information on the day-of-event.

During event

— Warn people ahead of time about the routes they should take.

— Advise of available options.

— Alert drivers about problems, delays and blockages.

— Suggest actions travellers should take.

Communication with the media should start before the event. If there is pre-event advice that stakeholders wish to disseminate, then the media can be a conduit to the public. During the event, the media can be used to provide real-time updates about transportation system delays and blockages. Again, advice on how to avoid the delays can be provided.

Most agencies already have some forms of communication in place with the media. However, these may not be the best way to communicate during the planned special event. For example, many agencies work with traffic reporting services during periods of recurring congestion. The planned special event may be taking place on a weekend or holiday when the traffic reporting service is not in service.

Alternate means to get real-time information to broadcasters may be needed. The media may also find that the usual means they use to get traffic information are unavailable during the planned special event. Due to security concerns, airspace near the site may be off limits. This makes the media more dependent upon the agencies to provide them with updates. Unless a proactive decision is made otherwise, most agencies would not want the media to call the command post for updates.

Calls to and from the TMC may be the best way to get information to the media. Wherever the media are directed to call, it is important that the person handling those calls has the most up-to-date, accurate information available. For the media to trust this source, they must believe that this is the best place to get information. Since most media want to verify information on their own, agencies should be prepared for the media to seek out other sources. The media may also acquire information via cell phones from event patrons driving to the planned special event, and the media will want to verify the information the public provides with the transportation agencies. If trust is lost between the media and the agencies, the agencies may lose control of the flow of information.

Dissemination of Traveller Information

Traveller information will have two important audiences during the event: (1) those who plan to attend and (2) those who want to avoid the delays the event may cause. In both cases, traveller information tools can be used to effectively disseminate information. Traveller information dissemination methods are:

— Newspapers and printed materials
— Radio and television
— Internet (e.g., websites and e-mail)
— Changeable message signs
— Highway advisory radio
— Telephone information systems

The dissemination of traveller information begins before the event with warnings of what may occur, preferred routes to the site and around it, and where drivers can get updates on the day-of-event. Different tools lend themselves to particular uses. Newspapers and other printed material, for example, lend themselves to graphic information such as maps. The Internet represents a powerful medium for disseminating pre-trip travel information to event patrons and other transportation system users.

Changeable message signs function best to raise awareness of a potential problem while road users are en-route, and highway advisory radio is somewhere in the middle, being able to provide more detail than signs, but less than printed material. The planned special event is likely to require the deployment of portable changeable message signs because a greater concentration of information is needed and because the event may be taking place in a location where permanent devices are not in place.

Portable highway advisory radio stations may also be considered to reach motorists. In planning for the event, stakeholders must consider: (1) which devices will be used, (2) approved messages that can be displayed, and (3) how to disseminate the information to event patrons and other transportation system users. No one system will reach all of the people that stakeholders wish to alert. In fact, even if all systems are used, operators will not reach every transportation system user.

But, by using a variety of tools, the traffic management team will be able to reach a critical mass of people so that delays will be minimised and the customer requirements of all users satisfied. On the day-of-event, it must be clear who will update traveller information devices and how timely and accurate information will get to the officials responsible for providing the updates. These individuals must be part of the communication chain. Again, assigning a dedicated person to handle the updates would be ideal. Conflicting priorities could result in out-of-date information being disseminated if one person is asked to handle too many tasks.

Traffic Monitoring

Traffic monitoring represents an important day-of-event activity, serving to provide traffic and incident management support in addition to performance evaluation data. Timely deployment of contingency plans developed during the event operations planning phase depends on the accurate collection and communication of real-time traffic data between traffic management team members.

Agencies responsible for managing planned special events require numerous types of information on the current conditions of the system to support delivery of effective service for the planned special event. This required information varies widely depending on: (1) the service being provided, (2) how often it needs to be collected, and (3) how accurate it needs to be. Information is crucial for successful operations of the transportation network.

In a traffic management system, the traffic monitoring component, or surveillance component, is the process in which data is collected in the field. This data is used to supply information about conditions in the field to other system components including personnel located in the field on the day-of-event. Functions of surveillance information are:

— Measure traffic and environmental conditions in real-time.

— Make control decisions.

— Disseminate traveller information.

— Monitor and evaluate system and plan performance.

Surveillance is not limited to collecting and monitoring traffic condition information alone, nor in some instances are they automated in nature. Surveillance is applied to weather and pavement conditions to provide operators and maintenance staff more information to support their traffic and transit management responsibilities. These systems also are being used to manage snow removal, icy roadway treatment, to detect limited sight distance problems caused by fog or smoke, and to detect high water levels along roadways.

While much traffic surveillance (detection) is accomplished via automated means, manual detection, most notably via in-field personnel on cell phones or two-way radios and cell-phone calls from motorists, is a viable and reliable strategy for planned special event management. In many instances of planned special event management, the surveillance must be microscopic rather than macroscopic, i.e., a particular point or location must be monitored rather than an area or region, and this strategy of manual detection is the most cost-effective and efficient. Various technologies that exist for collecting this information are described below.

— In-roadway and over-roadway sensors for measuring traffic flow parameters

— Vehicle probes for collecting data on travel times and origin-destination information

— Closed circuit television (CCTV) systems for viewing real time video images of the roadway

— Road weather information systems (RWIS) for gathering information on pavement and weather conditions

— Traffic signal and system detectors to measure congestion on streets

— Parking management systems to monitor available capacity in parking garages or lots

— Manual methods

Detection and surveillance, whether highly technical and automated or simple and manual, is the cornerstone of traffic monitoring. Traffic management strategies and Intelligent Transportation Systems (ITS) technologies can assist in reducing congestion, improving safety, and enhancing mobility. However, without the capability to know the current operating conditions, coupled with the cooperation and coordination among personnel in the responsible agencies, the potential benefits of these strategies and technology systems may not be realised. To that end, it is not a simple matter to quantify benefits from detection and surveillance alone, but instead to understand the benefits realised from traffic management strategies and ITS technologies that rely on detection and surveillance. Some benefits of detection and surveillance are:

— Reduction in delay and congestion related to early detection and verification of incidents.

— Reduction in secondary accidents as a result of early incident detection.

— Reduction on capital (e.g., salt) and recurring (e.g., plow crews) costs associated with snow and ice removal with the use of Remote Weather Information Sensor technology.

— Improved traveller information.

The information collected through the monitoring effort is valuable for post-event activities. After the event, the information gathered and/or observed can be used as part of the program or event evaluation. The data collected provides: (1) input into estimating the benefits of the traffic management plan and operation and (2) input into planning for future planned special events. An example of some statistics or measures that can be obtained from traffic monitoring on the day-of-event, and can commonly be used to evaluate the effectiveness of the event traffic management plan and operation includes:

— Reduction in delay

— Change in mode

— Increase in transit ridership

— Reduction of travel time

— Increase in travel speed

— Reduction in loaded cycle lengths at signalised intersections

Performance measures provide the basis for identifying the location and severity of problems (such as congestion and delay), and for evaluating the effectiveness of the implemented planned special event management strategies. In essence, performance measures are used to measure how the transportation system, and therefore the traffic management plan, performs with respect to the adopted goals and objectives, both for ongoing management and operations of the special event and the evaluation of future options. Use of traffic monitoring information are:

— Track changes in system performance during the event.

— Identify locations or corridors with poor performance.

— Identify potential causes and associated remedies (i.e., contingency plans).

— Identify specific areas that require improvement/ enhancements for future events.

— Provide information to decision-makers and the public.

— Provide input to post-event evaluation.

Most measures for planned special event management are congestion-based and are measures that can be quickly and efficiently assessed. Certainly other non-transportation measures are important to successful planned special event management; however, these are neither accurate nor timely enough to allow for day-of-event management. Some performance evaluation measures are listed below:

— Parking occupancy and turnover rate

— Arrival and departure service rate at parking area access points

— Time to clear parking lots

— Vehicle delay at intersections

— Queue length

— Travel time and delay on freeways and streets

— Traffic volume to capacity ratio

— Traffic speed

— Number and location of crashes and other incidents

— Traffic incident clearance time

Following are some of the reasons that agencies have instituted performance measures and the associated monitoring and evaluation processes.

— Provide better information about the transportation system to the public and decision makers (in part due, no doubt, to a greater expectation for accountability of all government agencies).

— Improve management access to relevant performance data.

— Improve agency efficiency and effectiveness, particularly where demands on the transportation agency have increased while available resources have become more limited.

In managing travel for planned special events, a direct relationship exists between the performance measures selected and the data needed in the performance measurement process. The data and information used in decision-making must be of high quality because the remedies have to be performed immediately. They must originate from reliable, consistent sources and meet the needs of the decision makers. Moreover, the decision makers must have confidence in the information, or it will not be used. The most common data problems are acquiring the required information in the exact form desired, and in ascertaining the quality of the data.

The "garbage in, garbage out" concept applies to the data used in a performance measurement system. If the data gathered are highly uncertain, then the conclusions drawn by converting those data into performance measures also will be highly uncertain and will have reduced value to interested stakeholders. For this reason, great care needs to be taken in data collection.

In reality, however, some things either cannot be measured accurately or cannot be measured accurately at an acceptable cost and in an acceptable timeframe. Transportation agencies need to consider the uncertainty introduced by inaccurate data when taking action based on their system of performance measures, especially in planned special event management, where the modifications have immediate, and possibly disastrous, results.

Post-event Management

Post-event evaluation may mark the final stakeholder activity for this special event, it should be considered as the first step in planning for the next planned special event. The programme planning phase utilises lessons learned and evaluation results from one planned special event to develop products, such as policies and regulations and permanent infrastructure deployment, for improving travel management for all planned special events occurring in a region.

No matter how thorough the traffic management plan, chances are excellent not everything happened as expected. Maybe it was an oversight or an unexpected glitch. Perhaps some elements worked better than expected, and it turns out that all the resources allocated were not needed. Whatever the case, the evaluation phase is where the plan should be compared with what actually happened and appropriate decisions be made as to what to do differently the next time. Even if the same planned special event was handled dozens of times previously, there are adjustments that can be made based on the most recent experience.

The first steps in the evaluation of the traffic management plan implemented for the planned special event take place during the event operations planning phase. Knowing ahead of time that a post-event evaluation will occur allows participants to make provisions for the review. In particular, this means collecting data during the event, which can be used as part of the review process. At a minimum, this would include data indicating how the system performed and a log of what took place during the event. Data collection activities also include surveying of event patrons and the public to get their perspective on how well elements of the traffic management plan worked. Table 1 summarises key post-event activities.

Table 1. Key post-event activities

Action
- Review measures of effectiveness identified in event operations planning phase. - Compile agency measures of effectiveness. - Compile performance evaluation data. - Conduct stakeholder participant debriefing. - Conduct event patron survey. - Conduct public survey. - Conduct a post-event debriefing meeting. - Prepare a post-event report.

Measures of Effectiveness (MOE)

Measures of effectiveness (MOEs) represent quantitative measures that give some insight into how effectively a unit is performing. MOEs are measures of activity that, while not reflecting performance directly, show workload and trends. To evaluate how well the traffic management plan worked, some form of measurement is necessary.

In addition to telling stakeholders how effective their plan was, the measurements provide transportation professionals the means to demonstrate to others, including the media and elected officials, how well the plan may have worked. There are two areas of effectiveness that should be measured, internal and external:

— Internal measures are actions taken by the traffic management team that may not be apparent to the public. For example, while the public would note a traffic incident being cleared, they would not be aware of the total number of traffic incidents handled.

- Examples of internal data, which can be measured.
- Internal measures are beneficial to stakeholders in helping them evaluate traffic management team activity.

The following are the measures of Internal Measures of Effectiveness :

- Number of messages displayed on changeable message signs
- Number of messages broadcast on highway advisory radio
- Number of traffic incidents handled
- Number of messages transmitted between stakeholders
- Number of traffic signal timing changes
- Number times a ramp(s) was closed and time/ duration of closure(s)

External measures are readily identifiable by the public during a planned special event. The volume of traffic on primary and alternate routes represent two examples.

External measures are clearly experienced by most spectators attending a special event and are factors most likely to be noted by the public.

External measures are likely to be viewed as more important by those outside the traffic management team, such as transportation system users and community interest stakeholders. The following are the measures of External Measures of Effectiveness:

- Volume of traffic on major routes
- Volume of traffic on alternate routes
- Volume of traffic entering and exiting the site and parking areas

— Hours of delay
— Number of event patrons and participants utilising transit to and from the event
— Travel times
— Modal split
— Average vehicle occupancy

Stakeholders may measure hours of delay by predefining what is considered congestion and noting how long the congestion lasts.

While external measures provide hard statistics to demonstrate the plan's effectiveness, softer measures may also be beneficial. A survey of attendees may show how effective they perceived the traffic management plan. Their level of satisfaction with ease of access, quality of traveler information, and other activities can provide insights into how the users of the system view the effectiveness of the plan that was implemented.

Before deciding what to measure, it is important to decide how to evaluate the traffic management plan and the performance of the traffic management team. This decision may be driven, in part, by difficulties experienced during previous planned special events, political considerations, or a need to demonstrate the value of particular tools used during the event.

Programme Planning Process Integration

The evaluation must be more than an afterthought to gain the maximum benefit from it. As part of the programme planning process, the evaluation should be considered from the initiation of the process through its conclusion. If the evaluation is being done for the first time, those who are putting the plan together have to look at the goals and then design the evaluation to measure whether the goals have been met. Even if they were done for another event, the results of those evaluations should be examined before the traffic management plan is designed. In the case of an unrelated event, there may be some lessons learned that could be applied to this new event. If this is a recurring event, previous evaluations would have more specific insights that can be applied.

Since evaluation will be taking place throughout the planning process and during the event itself, it is important that the evaluation steps, goals and objectives be established during the programme planning phase or early in the event operations planning phase for a specific planned special event. Finally, as the event concludes, it is also important that a mechanism be created to take what is learned in the evaluation of a specific planned special event and put it in a form that allows the evaluation results to be applied to future events.

Evaluation of Future Events

Whether the event is a one-time only happening or an annual occurrence, what has been learned through the evaluation can contribute toward proactively improving travel management for all planned special events occurring in a region. To be beneficial for future planned special events, the results of the evaluation should be documented and made accessible. In the case of a one-time only event, the evaluation may show both general and specific insights, which can be used for other future planned special events. These could include areas such as traveler information, interagency communications, and the planning process itself. For recurring events, a file providing the cumulative benefit of lessons learned will help sharpen the traffic management plan developed for each new occurrence. It is also important to remember that with recurring events, slight changes in circumstances will require modifications to the plan.

Participant Evaluation

Stakeholder debriefing

At the conclusion of the planned special event, a debriefing session should be held. The stakeholder debriefing is an opportunity to bring together those involved and impacted by the planned special event. In it, these individuals, and the groups they represent, can compare what the plan called for and what actually took place. They can also examine areas the plan may not have addressed but turned out to be issues in hindsight. All of those who were involved in creating the traffic management plan, as well as key people who played a role during the event itself, should be present for this session. This includes stakeholders forming the event planning team and traffic management team. The elements of a stakeholder debriefing as follows:.

- Introductions of individuals and the roles they played (if not obvious)
- Explanation that the debriefing is not designed to find blame for anything which may have gone wrong, but to identify areas of improvement for future planned special events
- Distribution of a chronology of the special event, preferably one which melds individual agencies' own chronologies
- Review of the timeline of events
- Discussion of other areas of concern
- Next steps to incorporate lessons learned

Stakeholders include anyone who had a role or was affected by the planned special event. This certainly includes the transportation and public safety professionals who developed the plan and were involved in its execution. However, other stakeholders also have a strong interest, even if they had no part in creating the plan. For example, businesses that may have been affected by the special event, due to closed roadways limiting access, are stakeholders with a strong financial stake in the event.

The debriefing process should involve those directly involved in traffic and parking management during the event. This includes traffic management team members stationed at the command post, at the transportation management centers (TMC), and in the field. While they may not be present at the debriefing session, the viewpoints of other stakeholders should also be considered during the debriefing process.

The debriefing should not be viewed as a "finger-pointing" or "blame" session. If it is perceived that way, stakeholders will tend not to be frank about any of their own shortcomings and will more likely focus on defending themselves. To ensure involvement of all relevant stakeholders and to encourage their candid comments, it should be made clear that the debriefing session is not a time to blame anyone for something which may have gone wrong during the event.

A log or chronology of what took place during the event should be used to guide the discussion. Ideally, this log will incorporate the activities of all stakeholders so the events can be seen in the light of other actions that took place on the day of event. This log may be kept by a representative at the command post or at the TMC. If a master log is not kept, individual agencies can share their own chronologies before the meeting and these can then be merged into a single document. During the event, end-of-day review meeting notes should be examined to focus on actual situations and modifications that were incorporated into the plan. The evaluation will compare the plan with what actually took place. Actions, whether considered good or bad, that deviated from the plan should be noted. It is not enough to simply note what was different than expected, but why it differed from the plan. Stakeholders should also be candid about what they would do differently based on their experience during the event.

If the planned special event is a recurring one, lessons learned should be documented so that when a traffic management plan is developed for the next event occurrence, the plan addresses past lessons learned. Even if the event represents a one-time activity, the lessons learned should still be documented. Many of the lessons may have application for the next planned special event and can be used in developing traffic management plans for similar planned special events or future events occurring at the same venue.

Patron survey

Although the goal is to keep traffic moving on all of the transportation facilities, the patrons are the ultimate customers of everyone involved in the traffic management of the planned special event. It is largely for their benefit the traffic management plan was created in the first place, and they are the ones likely to suffer the greatest consequences if the plan does not work. Therefore, the viewpoint of event patrons is needed if a credible evaluation of the plan is to be done.

It is impossible to question everyone who attended the event, but a survey of attendees will give insight into the patrons' opinions. Unless measuring statistics for use in future event travel forecasting, it is not necessary that a scientific survey be done either. What is important is that a cross-section of patrons be surveyed in order to identify common threads. For example, if a significant number of patrons say traveler information was inaccurate, it will become clear that aspect of the plan needs to be reexamined. The patron survey can take following forms:

— Comment cards event patrons can fill-out

— Surveyors who question attendees

Solicited and unsolicited e-mailed comments

The survey should be brief in order to encourage a response. Yes or no type questions are easily answered. Sample questions for possible inclusion in a patron survey include:

— Were you aware of any special travel information before the event?

— Did you find information provided en-route to the event (e.g., via signs, radio) helpful?

— Did you experience any unexpected problems approaching the venue?

— Do you have any suggestions or other comments you wish to offer?

Public survey

The public survey takes in a wider audience than the patrons. This includes those who may have been impacted by the planned special event even though they did not attend the event. Since this is a larger and more diverse group of stakeholders, it may be more difficult to identify and survey them. Methods for reaching the public include surveys in rest areas along alternate routes and approach routes to the event, solicitations via websites, and comments provided by phone and mail. Surveys may be mailed to homeowners and businesses in the area affected by the special event to solicit their opinions. Sample questions for possible inclusion in public survey include:

— Were you aware of the event before it took place?

— If you were aware of the event beforehand, would you have altered your plans based on that information?

- Did you change your plans or schedule as a result of the event?
- How would you evaluate the effectiveness of traffic management efforts for this event (poor, good, excellent)?
- Do you have any additional comments or suggestions based on your experience?

An effort must be made to collate all comments from widespread locations to be certain all input is considered. Specific outreach may be made to members of the public who were directly impacted by the event. Businesses, residents, and transit riders are a few of those who may have experienced impacts caused by the planned special event. Since these individuals can be found at easily identifiable locations, or perhaps actively participated in the review and comment of the traffic management plan during the event operations phase, it is easier to survey these stakeholders.

Post-event debriefing

A post-event debriefing should be held to review what took place. The purpose of the debriefing is to:

1) examine what took place,
2) compare it to what was expected to happen,
3) identify what worked well, and
4) determine areas of improvement for future planned special events.

Meeting organisation

Ideally, the post-event debriefing should be planned during the event operations planning phase and before the event takes place. If that does not happen, the debriefing should still be held, but it may be more difficult to get full participation by all involved stakeholders. The meeting should be scheduled at least a few days after the event, giving traffic management team members some time to absorb what took place during the event and an opportunity to put it into perspective. However, the meeting should not be delayed too long after the event so memories of what took place remain fresh.

The place and timing of the meeting should be such that maximum attendance is realised. Considerations should include: (1) the rotating schedules of those who may attend, (2) ease of access to the meeting location, and (3) potential conflicts with other events.

If there were significant interagency conflicts during the planning of the event, or during the event itself, a neutral location and moderator may improve dialogue during the meeting.

If these types of conflicts were not a problem, consideration should be given to having one of the traffic management team supervisors or incident commander lead the meeting. Whatever the case, the moderator should be skilled in involving all the participants and in digging into responses to get to the root of any stated problems.

If the traffic management plan included a transportation management center, there may also be some advantages to holding the meeting at the TMC.

Meeting agenda

It is important to remember that the post-event debriefing is not designed to be a time to blame individuals or agencies for what took place during the event. This should be reflected in the agenda developed for the meeting. It should clearly state the intended purpose of the meeting. This will help keep meeting attendees focused and provide added assurance that the meeting is designed to identify successes and lessons learned.

Stakeholders can agree on a general outline for the debriefing even before the event. This helps assure the debriefing covers topics of interest to all participants and not designed to be biased against any stakeholder. Further details of the agenda can be filled in after the event and when problems requiring closer examination can be identified. Again, it would be beneficial if all participants had input into revising the agenda to make certain all concerns are addressed. The broad topic areas that should be covered in the post-event debriefing as follows:

— Purpose of meeting

— The planning process

— Interagency communications

— Traffic management in and around the venue

— Traffic management outside of the event site

Traveler information, including media

The purpose of the post-event debriefing is not to just identify what could have been done better but to note what was successful. As has been the case from the start of the event operations planning process through the event itself, multiple viewpoints are helpful as stakeholders identify key successes and lessons learned. Depending upon perspective, one element of the plan may be viewed as a success by one party and seen as an area needing improvement by another.

Identifying these areas can be accomplished as each stakeholder individually reviews its actions leading up to and going through the event and as the stakeholders, as a group, review what took place. It is helpful if participants are asked to identify, before the post-event debriefing, what they see as key successes and lessons learned. It may also prove beneficial if these notes are shared among the participants before the meeting to help facilitate discussion.

While identifying these points are very useful, it has little value unless there is some way to identify how to apply what is learned to the next planned special event. No one individual should be expected to serve as either the group's or their agency's corporate memory. The successes and lessons learned must be chronicled so that those stakeholders who are responsible for planning the next planned special event will be able to tap the wisdom of those who have done this before.

Post-Event Report

Table 2 presents an outline of a typical post-event report.

Table 2. Outline of Post-Event Report
Report Organisation

Report Organisation
- Outline report topics.
- Document products of the event operations planning phase.
- Identify key successes.
- Present lessons learned.
- Identify improvements for future events.
- Configure to serve as a working document for future special event planning.
- Review chronologically what took place.
- Summarise both positive and negative aspects.
- Include all stakeholder viewpoints.

Operational Cost Analysis

Operational Cost Analysis
- Examine operational costs.
- Include staffing, overtime, and equipment for each involved agency.
Identify potential cost savings
— Reallocation of personnel

— Division of responsibilities

— Use of technology

- Include total staffing, overtime, and equipment for all agencies.

Qualitative Evaluation

Qualitative Evaluation
- Include survey of stakeholders. - Include survey of event patrons. - Include survey of public.

Quantitative Evaluation

Quantitative Evaluation
- Provide numerical picture of the event. — Costs — Hours saved — Traffic incidents handled — Passengers carried on various modes. - Present cost/benefit analysis.

Report organisation

A report that reviews the planned special event is necessary to document what was learned. By clearly outlining the material in the report, it becomes easier to identify the key successes and lessons learned. It also makes it easier to go back to the report and look at particular aspects of the traffic management plan implemented when planning the next planned special event.

Since the process of handling the planned special event follows a timeline, the easiest way to organise the report may involve reviewing what took place chronologically. An alternative method of organising the report concerns dividing it by subject areas such as traffic management, traveler information, command center operation, and communications. Since some areas overlap, there should be references in the report to other sections, which may have application in multiple areas.

The report should summarise both positive and negative aspects. Remember, this is not designed to be a public relations piece to promote the handling of the planned special event but a working document to assist future special event planning. If differing perspectives are noted during the debriefing process and there is not consensus on how to address a particular situation, all stakeholder viewpoints should be documented.

As with the post-event debriefing, the post-event report should not blame individuals or organisations for anything that did not go well. The report should provide a factual recounting of the special event, including planning the event itself and what took place during the post-event debriefing. If opinions are noted in the report, then the opinions should be segregated from the factual information and noted as opinions. The elements of a post-event report are follows:

- A copy of the original traffic management plan
- A combined chronology of the event, incorporating actions by all participants
- List of recommended improvements
- Statistical information (e.g., number of traffic incidents, number of CMS and HAR messages).
- Survey results
- General comments by participants

Management of operational cost

Part of the evaluation process is to look at the operational costs of managing the planned special event. Expenses such as staffing, equipment and overtime should be noted by the agency incurring the expense. This information should be broken down into categories that allow others to understand the costs and the specific efforts associated with the expenditures. In the same way, operational decisions can be reviewed to identify areas that can be improved. Operational costs can also be reviewed with areas of potential cost saving identified. In some cases, these expenses may be in areas where the reallocation of personnel would result in reduced expenses or improved operations. In other areas, the use of technology may result in savings.

While individual stakeholders are responsible for gathering information on their own costs, there is also benefit in merging the figures of all agencies to have a better picture of total expenses for personnel and equipment. This may also provide opportunities to see how dividing responsibilities in different ways could result in cost savings. Among the costs that should be analysed are overtime expenses, costs of deploying equipment, equipment rental costs, additional communications expenses, and expenses for public information efforts.

Qualitative measures

The qualitative evaluation, while based on softer measures such as opinion and perspective, still provides a very valuable measure of the success in handling the planned special event. This is especially true when measuring patron and public views on the event. Quantitative measures may be easier to manage, but qualitative judgments may help determine the success of the plan. Even if the numbers show the plan was a success, if the qualitative evaluation shows significant dissatisfaction, it will be difficult to view the event in a positive light.

The qualitative evaluation is based on a number of factors, including the survey of the public and event patrons. Also important is the qualitative evaluation provided by those stakeholders who managed the event. If they view the exercise as a failure, it will be difficult to get them to fully commit to subsequent efforts for future planned special events. The followin are the key topics of a qualitative evaluation.

— Quality of pre-event information

— Quality of day-of-event information

— Direction provided to the event and at the venue

— Traffic management at the site

— Egress from the venue

Quantitative evaluation

The quantitative evaluation provides a numerical picture of the event. Figures such as costs, hours saved, incidents handled, and passengers carried provide a view which can be compared with similar events and provide a metric to judge how well the traffic management plan worked. As the saying goes, what gets measured gets done. If that is the case, then involved stakeholders should identify, before the event, what they wish to measure. While computer programmes allow any number of items to be tabulated and measured, a good understanding before the event will facilitate the measurement of the key areas identified.

The quantitative evaluation is very useful when conducting a cost/benefit analysis of activities for the planned special event. Knowing where the most benefit was realised for the costs incurred can help in the planning process to see if resources should be reallocated for the next event.

12

Event Marketing

Event marketing is a new way of marketing products, and since there is not much written about it, the definitions that can be found vary to a great extent. Event Marketing is an attempt to coordinate communication around an self-created or sponsored event. The event is an activity that gathers the target group in time and room, a meeting where a message is communicated and a happening is created. This definition is general and can be used for different kinds of events. However, depending on the objective of the event, the definition will change.

From the sponsor's perspective, common objectives of holding an event are to sell more products, to change and build image of a product, or to increase floor traffic. The word event can also have different meanings depending on how you define it. It could be a happening, an occurrence, or an incident. However, the core of Event Marketing is to give the customer a positive experience in connection with the products. In the United States where Event Marketing has been used the longest and it has been developed more than in other countries, it is possible to see some trends for what products it has been used for most.

These are image products, which mean liquor, cigarettes, cars, fashion, sport products, games, makeup, credit cards and some products from banks and airlines. Event Marketing is generally used in the introduction, or in the growth stage of the product life cycle. It is also often used when organisations are launching new products, or are trying to reach a new target group. Usually, the main purpose of an event is to create, enforce or sustain the corporate image of the organisation. This is created by how the attendees experience how the organisation manifests itself in the event, and it also depends on what relevance it has to the attendees individual and collective identities.

Event Marketing tries to give and catch the customer experiences. If the customer has a good experience in connection with the product it will make the relationship between customer and organisation stronger. This could be done in two ways, first through the customer and the organisation seeing each other "face to face", and secondly through the fact that when something is experienced, it stays in the memory for a longer time. However, it is important to remember that this works both ways. If something goes wrong during the event, the customer will remember this for a long time too.

The main concepts of Event Marketing are message, interaction and integration. The purpose of Event Marketing is to communicate a message through a planned happening. This also creates something valuable for the customer, and it does not only communicate it as it can do while using other marketing tools. The target group at the event gathers everyone at a specific time, in a specific place, and the success is built upon how involved customers are in the social gathering that is created. It also depends on whether the customer is at the event at her/ his own will or if the event happened to be where the customer is. There needs to be an interaction between the customer and the event.

Luttorp explains that Event Marketing should not be a separate event for the organisation but a complement to the marketing strategy; it should be integrated with the marketing strategy. Milgrom also discusses how important it is for the marketers to use Event Marketing as part of both the marketing strategy and the overall business strategy.

Event marketing refers to an ongoing programme of educational events that demonstrate your firm's expertise and position in your market. It can do more than increase short-term traffic and sales. Properly planned and promoted, special events create long-term results far out of proportion to the events themselves. Event marketing helps you:

— *Build awareness*: You can enhance your firm's awareness without cutting prices (and profits) with a "sale."

— *Create and reinforce relationships*: Events give you an opportunity to prove your competence to prospects and a reason to recontact past customers, renewing your acquaintance and showing appreciation for their patronage.

— *Arouse excitement*: Event marketing creates anticipation among customers, prospects, and your sales staff.

— Establish deadlines for completing promotional projects, like newsletters, renovations, or a special report.

— *Attract the press*: Educational events are more likely to result in favourable media coverage than price-oriented sales or promotions.

Opportunities are limited only by your imagination. Choose from among:

— Customer appreciation days. Invite customers in for a free, non-selling, cup of espresso, a concert, or a harbour cruise combined with an open house.

— "Challenges and opportunities" presentations. Invite customers and prospects to a review of current economic and technological trends, and your analysis of their probable impact.

— Demonstrations and workshops make it easy to introduce new products and services in an editorial, or case study, as opposed to a "sales" environment.

— Teleclasses. Teleclasses offer you an opportunity to promote your expertise and competence to distant prospects.

The number of people who attend your event is not as important as what happens before, during, and after the event. Quality of response and follow-up are usually more important than attendance.

Event Planning

Begin by asking: "What type of event is most appropriate to the goal I want to accomplish?" Next, create a deadline planner. Work backwards from the date of your event. Deadline planners help you set up and maintain a realistic promotion schedule that covers all bases. Your deadline planner should specify each of the tools you're going to use to promote your event, including ads, letters, postcards, e-mail, and your web site-as well as local calendar listings.

Invite attendees to call or e-mail you to confirm their intention to attend. Try to obtain all attendees' e-mail addresses. Send registered attendees an e-mail reminder a few days before the event as well as the morning of the event. You can also review directions and instructions for attendees as well as attach an advance copy of audience handouts.

During the event, keep track of who attended and give attendees meaningful handouts. Prepare and collect evaluation sheets that invite comment. These testimonials will reinforce the impact of the event and boost attendance at future events. Hire a professional photographer to take pictures for you and the media. At the end of the event, hold a drawing for door prizes-perhaps contributed by your marketing partners or vendors.

After the event, always say thank you! Send participants a "Thank you for attending" postcard or e-mail the next day. Post pictures on your web site. Later, send a follow-up mailing summarising highlights of the event to those who attended and those who should have.

New Demands on Marketing

Event Marketing is not a new concept, and different forms of events have always been around. Sponsorship and Event Marketing are the world's fastest growing forms of marketing. Corporate giants are spending millions of dollars on naming rights for everything from sporting complexes, to arenas, fairs, and festivals. The real start of sponsorship was during the Olympics 1994. According to the International Events Group, the definition of Event Marketing is: "promotional strategy linking a company to an event, sponsorship of a sports competition, festival etc."

Sometimes it is used as a synonym for "sponsorship," but not all sponsorships involve an event. Event Marketing gathers people around events that can be everything from a small happening with few attendees to a long chain of happenings involving thousands of people. The target group can be the end customer, business representatives, or the internal employees of the company. The events can be anything from kickoffs, launching of new products, product presentation, and sponsoring.

Events can have many different purposes, but the most common one is to get attention and to create an image for a specific brand, or for the whole organisation, build brand awareness and increase customer sales. Some organisations use Event Marketing in their marketing strategy to support nonprofit organisation as "good cause marketing".

Another purpose of Event Marketing could be to inform about new features on existing products or brand new products. This can be done not only by the use of the Event, but also by using the media attention around an event. Event Marketing is part of the marketing strategy. It is an integrated marketing tool included in the marketing mix. Today's business climate demands that sales and marketing executives place greater importance on quantifiable results.

Five Ps of Marketing

The five Ps of marketing: product, place, people, price and promotion play an essential role in Event Marketing. To successfully use Event Marketing the marketer must understand how Event Marketing fits together with the other parts of the marketing strategy. Kotler describes the organisation's marketing mix as controllable variables that are mixed so that the organisation gets the response that they are asking for from the target market. Event Marketing fits under promotion in the marketing mix.

Event Marketing is not a substitute for any of the other components- it is a complement. If an organisation uses Event Marketing, they still need to use the other parts of the promotion mix before, during, and after the event. An example of this could be how a car producer can have advertisements to inform about a new car launch, and then use events to get people to test drive the new car, and then follow up with direct marketing with a discount coupon.

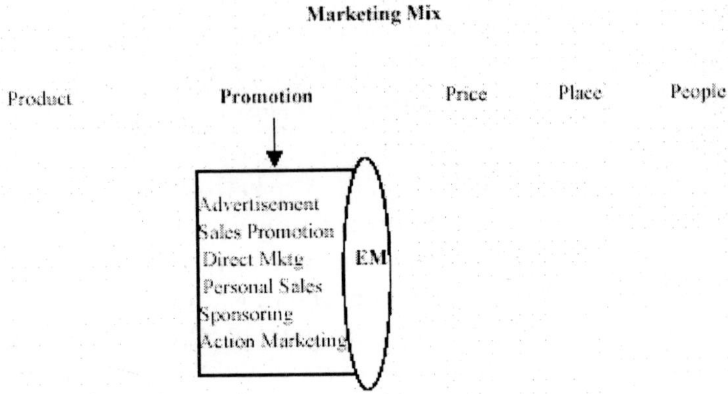

Figure 1. Marketing mix vs. Event Marketing.

One of the main advantages with Event Marketing compared to the other channels is that the objective can both be direct sales, and image building, depending on how it is used.

Effects of Communication

Communication is the process of moving a message that includes different elements. Those elements include source, message, channel, receiver and the process of encoding and decoding. The source is the organisation, the message could be a new car launch, the channel could be the event, and attendees are the receivers. A problem many marketers have is to make sure that the noise that can disturb the message going from the sender to the receiver does not interfere with the message, and thereby influence the effect it has on the customer.

The direct communication with the customer is one of the main advantages with Event Marketing compared to other marketing channels. In the definition of Event Marketing, it is said that "an event is an activity that gathers the target group in time and room." This means that the event is eliminated from the noise. Event Marketing is marketing communication in four different dimensions.

The Communication Process in traditional marketing.

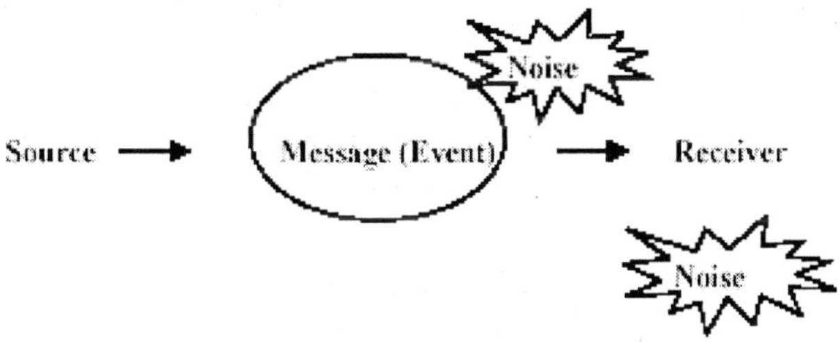

Figure 2. Communication Process in Event Marketing

The first one is the emotional communication method. The Event Marketing is a form of "pull" marketing, where the organisations try to get closer to the feelings and emotions of the customers. They do this not by "pushing" their products at the customers, but by touching the customers' emotional feelings.

The second dimension touches the customers by involving them in activities. When the customer gets a feeling from a product, he/she is informed of the value of the product. An example of this in the car industry is the test-driving of new cars.

The third dimension is the intellectual dimension and it regards the relevance of the event for the customers.

The fourth dimension is the spatial dimension, how to get the three prior dimensions into action and to inform the customers through all marketing channels.

Some researchers say that in the future, customers will not buy just the product, but the meaning, the event, and the character, which in turn give the customers the possibility to create their own value for the product.

Sponsorship and Event Marketing

However, there are many other marketing tools that can build brand-awareness, and create image and not confuse them with event marketing the most common confusion will be explained here. Authors seem to mix up the concept of Event Marketing and sponsorship, although there is a difference between the two. When using Event Marketing, the organisation works with the event as part of the marketing strategy. When sponsoring an event, the organisation buys exposure during the event at different levels of the event itself.

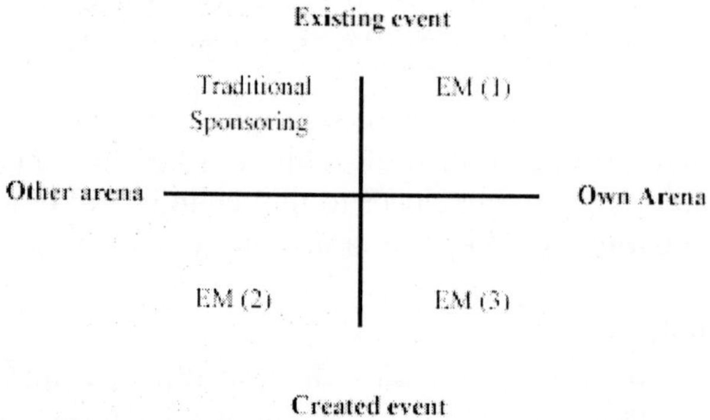

Figure 3. Traditional sponsoring vs. Event Marketing.

International Events Group (IEG) defines sponsorship this way: "The relationship between a sponsor and a property in which the sponsor pays a cash or in-kind fee in return for access to the exploitable commercial potential associated with the property." By using the commercial right, the sponsor could associate the brand and have an effective selection of the target group to market themselves to. The association makes the brand synonymous with the sponsored happening, and thereby the sponsoring has been called association by event.

Today sponsorship is one of the world's fastest growing forms of marketing, and together with Event Marketing they begin to play a more dominant role in many companies' marketing budgets. This model shows one way to look at where traditional sponsoring fits in compared to Event Marketing. When the organisation is sponsoring an event, (upper left corner), there is always a business agreement between at least two parties, which Event Marketing does not necessarily have. Usually this is the case when there is a sport competition such as the Olympics or a World Championship. This kind of sponsoring limits the possibilities for the organisation to market their products since they have no control over the happenings at the event, etc. There is a concept called the double lever effect, which explains the relationship between different events.

When organisations move to EM (1), (2) and (3) the organisations increase their control and also the risk is increased. When the control is increased, there is also a larger possibility for organisations to use the event integrated with the other marketing strategies. This figure shows how it comes to be a double lever effect:

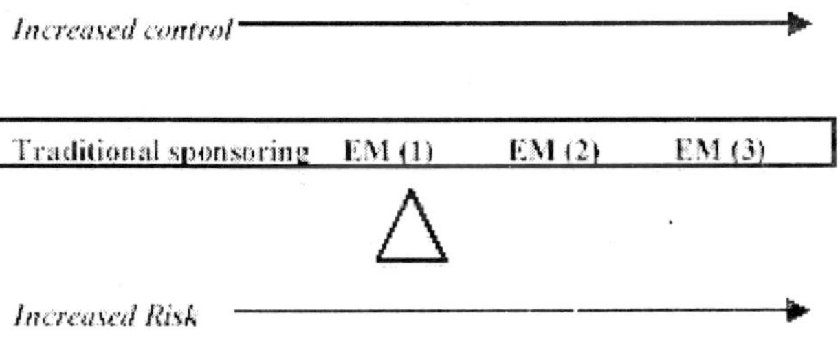

Figure 4. Control, and risk depending on activity.

As we can see, there is a risk in using Event Marketing. There is no possibility to test the event for the target group, and everything has to work during the event. The risk associated with the event could be one of the reasons why some organisations choose to use pre-existing events instead of own events. Preexisting events are events that are created by someone else for another purpose.

Categories of Event Marketing

Event Marketing could be used in many different ways. Depending on the objectives, some are more suitable than others. The main objectives for using Event Marketing are to create a relationship between the buyer and the organisation, to build brand-awareness, and to change or build an image of the product. D'Astous & Bitz use four different categorisations of events depending on the objective. An event could be either philanthropic or commercial. The philanthropic is supported by a cultural or social cause.

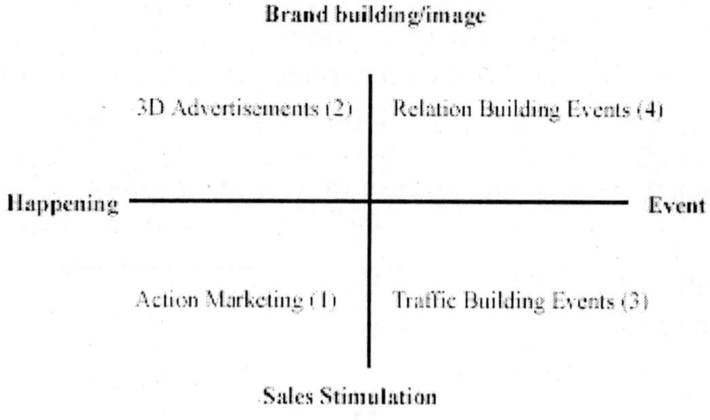

Figure 5. Categorisation model.

Usually, philanthropic events are just sponsored by the organisation while it is created and owned by a non-profit organisation. Depending on the objective the use of commercial events could be more valuable for an organisation. According to research done by D'Astous & Bitz, philanthropic events have a more positive impact on the perceptions of the sponsor's image than commercial events. However, Armstrong argues that media coverage of philanthropic events is usually smaller than that of commercial events.

Action Marketing is not Event Marketing by definition, but the two concepts go hand in hand. Action Marketing can be used for events that create direct sales. It is used in the last step in the buying process, when the actual decision is taken to buy the product or not. The differences between Sales Promotion and Action Marketing are that Action is a name that gathers all activities that stimulate direct sales.

By definition Action Marketing (AM) is a creative form of sales promotion. 3D advertisement is also not Event Marketing by definition. This is the concept of when the organisation has created creative billboards or other message carriers where they can gain plenty of attention, which is its only similarity to Event Marketing. Those happenings take place in an environment, unnatural for the product, and require an active consumer. Usually, those billboards get lots of attention in media, just as Event Marketing can get, and they have a news value.

Traffic Building Events are events have the objective to gather the target group in time and room, and should try to create a meeting between attendees and organisation. It may be possible for two totally different organisations to work together to try to develop a joint event. Usually the customers at these events are not there only to see, or experience the product, but to buy groceries or something else at the same time.

The main purpose of Relation Building Events on the other hand, is to build relations with the customer. The events are emotional and involve the customer in a specific way. Normally when the customer is attending a Relation Building Event, the event is the main activity rather than the place where the event is held. Relation Building Events are connected to Relationship Marketing (RM). Relationship Marketing is an organisation's effort to develop a long-term, costeffective link between customers for mutual benefit. Relationships are not easily achieved, and they can not be bought. It takes both time and strategy to capture the habits and individual preferences of the customers.

Relation- Building Events have the purpose of creating relationships between the organisation and customers. It could be used both for business-to-business as well as business-to-customer. At the business-to-customer events, there are often more attendees, larger groups and the groups are less defined as when the events are for business-to-businesses. Relationship events can also be used as internal events for the organisation.

Relation building events is an attempt for the organisation to enforce the image of the organisation or product. One of the differences between relation-building events and other types of events is that the relation-building events are emotional and involve the customer in a specific way. Some researchers do not agree that the event itself build relations, saying that the event is just a communication tool and that it is easier to collect information about the customers at an event than by using other communication tools. According to them, this is the main reason why an organisation has events.

Projects

The general assumption about project work theories is that it is applicable to all kinds of projects in all kinds of environments and industries. The outcomes of the projects, and the knowledge required for the project could differ; but the physical structure, planning, controlling and leading management around the project is still assumed to be similar for all projects. There are few theories written about evaluation of Event Marketing, therefore theories about project work have been used to see if they can be implied for Events as well.

There are many different definitions of a project. According to Keeling a project is "a temporary endeavour undertaken to create a unique product or service." It includes a limited time span, a target date for completion, and an outcome different from that produced in the course of operational routine. Also a project is "by its nature unique", i.e. it has few routine components and the work therefore has to break new ground or provide new insight for participants and stakeholders. In doing so, the project introduces both an element of risk and a certain degree of challenge for those involved.

"A project is often a cross-disciplinary orientation, combining different professional views and knowledge in one operational, goal-directed concept." Project Management has become a generic word for all theories applicable to project work. Like most definitions, there are elements in the definition of project work that could be questioned. However, most definitions state that a project is a given unique task, limited in time, complex in its implementation and subject to evaluation.

The event is also a planned happening that is limited to a specific time. No event is similar to another event, it is unique, and it is a risk to arrange an event if it is not successfully done, and it goes through different stages. Projects have reached new heights of sophistication and popularity during the last decade. Since it has become a trend to use projects, people use the term for everything that needs to be done within an organisation, which is not correct. Many organisations use project work as their regular method of doing businesses.

Projects are according to Lundin & Söderholm, almost always motivated "by a need to perform specific action." They also say that former literature of project work emphasises action as an important factor for the success of a project. When defining projects, it is important to differentiate them from other organised settings in the organisation. Projects can have short duration, be inexpensive or they can be ambitious undertakings over many years. However, Keeling states that most projects have some things in common: they are separate undertakings, they have discrete purpose and objectives, and they are of limited duration.

Also most projects have target dates for commencement and completion, their own resource, and their own management and management structure. Lundin and Söderholm mention four important concepts that they believe help to define a project. These four are time, task, team and transition. The four concepts work together and are dependent on each other. The permanent organisation is defined more by goals, survival, working organisation and production process. Time is one of the aspects that differentiate projects from permanent organisations.

You can often hear that the project is "temporary" or "limited in time." These aspects are well known before the project starts, and time can be regarded as a scarce resource. Also, you can look at time divided into past and future, how time is adding to the past and subtracting from the future. For a project, time is always running out, since it is limited from the start. There are some crucial aspects to consider in regards to time. There is a need for time schedules, synchronisation and allocation of time to avoid uncertainty and conflict resolution.

A project deals with time as a scarce, linear and valuable tool. This means that the project usually has a beginning, middle and an end. The task legitimises the project. In permanent organisations, you work towards a goal and in temporary organisation and projects, you work towards a task. The task is of major importance since the people working in the project are motivated by the task. It has been found that the task is more motivating to people working in projects than the goal is for someone working in an organisation.

There are, according to Lundin and Söderholm, two different types of tasks, the unique and the repetitive. All projects are designed by and around a team. The team's attitudes, beliefs and expectations will influence the teamwork, it is common that personal attributes will affect the project work. The team is always formed around the task of the project, the participation in a team is predefined as time-limited, and the people working in the team have other "homes" that they go back to when the project work is done.

Stages

Since time is usually conceived to be in linear form there is a beginning, middle and an end of a project, just as there is for an event. Projects can be divided into different stages depending on how you look at them. Lundin and Söderholm suggest four stages as the figure shows. Packendorff however suggests that there are three stages for a project: development, implementation and termination. He also describes that the development stage can be divided into two other stages, implementation and termination.

However, according to Lundin and Söderholm, the first step, the conceptualisation is the starting point, where the need for a development is recognised. The preliminary goals are discussed, and ideas about budget, and ways to approach the project. In this stage it might also be time to seek approval for the project by sub ordinaries or other parties that might be affected by the project. In the next step, the development or planning phase the ideas and objectives will have received initial considerations. The staff for the project will be selected and the objective, project structure and components of the project will be decided upon.

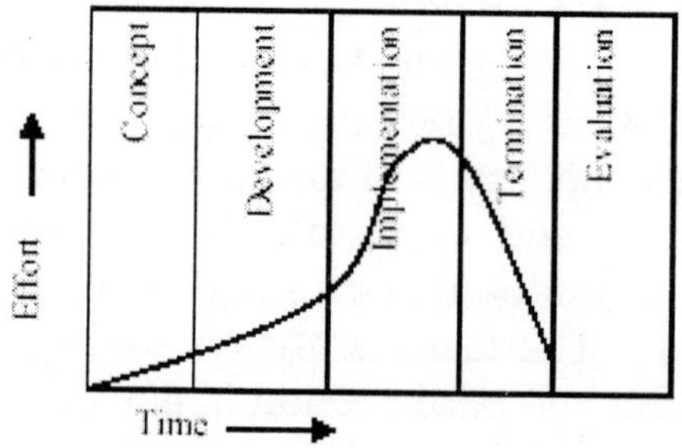

Figure 6. The four basic phases of a project's life cycle.

In the implementation stage the execution of the project will be conducted. This is when the plan is actually put into operation. The outcome of the work will be directly related to the result of the planning, development phase. In the termination phase, the completion of the project will be done. Most researchers agree that the project is developed stage by stage, and usually a project is discussed in accordance with different phases that it passes through. Keeling however points out an additional stage, called the evaluation stage. He says that during the process, the evaluation confirms the results and defines the base on which further progress will be built. It can help to make minor or major adjustments to keep the project on straight roads to its objectives.

Theoretical Framework

Complexity of Evaluation

By understanding the definition of a project and the Event

Marketing, it is easier to see the link between the two concepts. It is important to understand that there is not one single performance-evaluation theory that can be used for all projects, and thereby all events. All projects need different evaluation tools and techniques, although there are some aspects that are common for all of them. Project Management is about the future, and evaluation is about studying the past. One can ask oneself why be bothered about evaluating the past at all. One should keep in mind however that evaluation offers a basis for the development of project expertise.

Some people believe that it is impossible to evaluate Event Marketing, but according to Behrer and Larsson this is not correct. They believe that it can be measured to the same extent as other marketing channels, and that it can be measured with the same instruments that are used for evaluating other marketing tools. According to Lieungh, only the largest organisations measure their events. He believes that the reason why Event Marketing is not being measured by all organisations depends on lack of time, short-timeobjectives, ignorance, bad placement, and that many business leaders are too conservative.

Getz et al. also talk about how events include both tangible and intangible aspects that are much harder to evaluate. The intangible aspects could be experiences of the customers attending the event, as well as how the weather was during the event. Since the experience aspect is both produced and consumed simultaneously it is very difficult to control. What is important to consider is that some things are possible to measure, as impressions and media equivalencies, but it might not be what really matters for the organisation.

What really matters might instead be the tangible aspects as shareholder value and return on investment. The large Event Agency in America, International Event Group considers these areas most important to evaluate.

According to Jerkedal, one definition of project evaluation is "to describe and value a programme." Evaluation of a project is a process that extends throughout the project life cycle. During the planning phase of the project, it should be discussed how the evaluation and monitoring of the project should be performed. The planning for the evaluation is as important as the planning for the project.

There are some key requirements that should be considered when planning the evaluation. According to Cleland, these are "the inclusion of an evaluation policy and the process, the commitment of all key managers involved in the project to an evaluation strategy for evaluation methodologies, and the use of both inside and independent evaluators who have the professional credentials to do a credible job of the evaluation process." Getz also argues that the evaluation of the event should be thought of already in the planning phase of the event.

There needs to be extensive planning in order for an organisation to successfully use Event Marketing, and to successfully evaluate the event. Keeling also discusses that evaluation methods vary between all projects. It can consist of a financial statement, comparison of planned and actual results, effectiveness of remedies, communication and control procedures. There are as many evaluation techniques as there are projects. However, in the final review of a project the evaluation can be very detailed, including financial statements, audit reports, comparison of results to objectives and to old projects.

Direct Marketing is considered to be a measurable marketing tool. It is marketed through different medias directly to the customers and it builds longterm customer relationships. Since the response is direct, it is possible to measure. Direct-marketing can personalise and customise the message more than other marketing tools. Some of the most common ways of using direct marketing is through catalogue sales; by using specific mailing lists etc.

Important of Evaluating Event Marketing

Behrer & Larsson believe that the reason why some people think that it is not possible to evaluate events is that they have used Event Marketing without a specific purpose or objective. Hoyle argues that the cornerstone in the evaluation of events lies in the objective of the event. Event Marketing can have different objectives, and it is usually not directly to increase direct sales. Whatever the goal is, the easiest one to evaluate is the one that is expressed and quantified. The most common criteria for a goal to be valid is that it has a time limit, is challenging, measurable, realistic, result oriented, clear and that it could be followed.

If the goal is challenging, it is more interesting to try to reach it. If it is too, simple it is not inspiring to work for, but at the same time it has to be realistic. Time limit and measurable goals give a possibility to do a qualitative study. It is important that they are clear so that everyone understands them and that they can easily be followed by developing a strategy for how to reach them. Lööw believes that the goal should be stated in written form, and that the main goal should be broken down into smaller parts. She says that it is important to understand the main goal as well as the smaller parts.

The Process oriented evaluation looks into, follows, and observes what the programme has accomplished, and the Goal-Free Evaluation is a complement to the other forms of evaluation. The evaluator should try to look behind the goals with curiosity, to see what the results of the project are. The Goal-related evaluation method is the behavioural evaluation method. This methods looks into how well the objectives of the project have been reached. The objectives are of course very project specific.

It can be hard to measure some objectives such as the objective is to have "broaden horizon." The way to measure this is to have lots of smaller objectives, more specific on the way. Purpose of evaluation It is important that people know why the evaluations are performed, and that they know how they can use the results. Before doing an evaluation it is important to know its purpose. It can both be to control someone or something, and to legitimise an action.

According to Nordberg, the only relevant reason for doing an evaluation is to see how the project can be used in the future development of projects. He also says that it is important to know exactly what you want to evaluate before doing it. Meeuwisse describes that if the evaluation is done by an external researcher, there are not only different purposes with the evaluation, but there might also be different expectations on what the evaluation will find out. Some researchers might also have their own interests in the evaluations that need to be considered.

There are many different ways to look at evaluation. When evaluating a project in a rational world, you try to find out if the change that the project has created is worthwhile. This question cannot be answered without a type of criterion. This criterion is the goal or objective of the project. Christensen and Kreiner on the other hand describe project evaluation in an incomplete world vs. in a complete world.

They argue that the genuine insecurity of the project will make it impossible to do a traditional evaluation of a project built on scientific tools. They think that the regular "look back" evaluation should be replaced by an evaluation of the future value for the organisation; that it is part of the evaluation process to develop the final objective. They think that the goals should be floating and vague during the project work, since that will create opportunities for the people involved to develop their own view of interest.

When looking at evaluation through this point of view, the actual results, in regards to the success or failure of the project, are evaluated through a social process. They continue by saying that it is not the past performance of the past project phases that are decisive for the success or not, it is the modern, up to date social understanding and definition process. According to this, the evaluation is not to document the effectiveness of the project, but to judge the value of the result of the project.

In this way, the project itself is not a success or failure, but it will be a success or failure as a result of the evaluation process. The difference between this way of looking at evaluation and the traditional way can be described by the following definitions, traditional: "We know the target with our project, and the evaluation will show us to which extent we attained what we wanted," and Christensen and Kreiner: "We know what we attained, and the evaluation will decide what we actually attained with it."

Returning event

A returning event is an event that is being conducted as a series of events. It might not be the exact same event, and the attendees might not be the exact same one, but the arrangement around the event is very similar to previous events. According to Keeling, the evaluation can be a comparison with: other projects by the same organisation, the operation of similar processes in other fields of work, the work and results of competitors, equipment suitability, operating conditions, reliability performance and value. Hoyle explains that an advantage with events that are re-occurring is that they can be measured by comparing them with previous events, whereby their development can be measured.

Identity, Image, Positioning vs. Evaluation

Event Marketing is often used to create brandawareness,

image and identity for the products. Event Marketing can have both a communicative as well as a teaching approach for the customer.

Identity

Identity is what the organisation wants to stand for. The differences between identity and image are that identity is as mentioned earlier what the franchiser intends to represent, while the image is how the consumers experience the brand. The Image is on the receiver's side, while the identity is on the sender's side. Image focuses on how certain groups perceive a product or brand and refers to the way these groups decode the signals transmitted by the product service and communication of the brand. The purpose of identity, on the other hand, is to specify the brand's meaning, aim and self-image.

In regards to Event Marketing it could be said that the organisation sends away an Identity at the event and the customers receive it as an image of the product or organisation.Using Event Marketing can also differentiate the product for the customer by making the value of the brand stronger for the customer's identity. Identity comes from Latin and means "same". The identity for a customer means, "who am I in regards to the surroundings, and to myself?" The brand of a product can symbolise a part of the individual customer's identity. The brand can create a promise for the customer, and the product gives the brand the physical proof of that promise.

The event in Event Marketing can be seen as a value community. In regards to Maslow's thoughts, humans have needs that need to be satisfied. The Value community creates groups, where three concepts for group development need to be filled in order to create group belonging. Event Marketing can offer the individual a short-track to belonging by letting the individual attend an event. Through the event, the happening and the message will give the individual a picture of him/herself, and a sense of belonging with other individuals. This shows that part of the brand advantages lies in the possibility to influence the individual's identity, and to make possible his/her relation to other individuals and in this way strengthen their value community. By doing this, there is a possibility to differentiate the brand from other brands.

The brand is seen as an independent method of competition. A way to evaluate the Identity of an organisation can be by using a qualitative study. Evaluating a project means that the organisation keeps track of and systematically check all projects' activities and examines and appraises how things are going with the project. This could, according to Cleland, be developed into a control function with four different steps. The first two steps are concerned with what information to gather about the project and the actual collecting of the information. The collecting of information would be a qualitative study of what is actually happening. An example of this could be how the technique used during the project is performing, and what the cost for the project is.

The other steps in the control function are concerned with comparing the information gathered, and corrective action that should be taken. Qualitative information on the project can be gathered in both a formal and an informal way. The formal way is by reports, briefings, counts etc, and the informal way is by observations or it can take the form of a simple conversation with attendees. The importance of the qualitative study is to know what information needs to be gathered. During the participant observation the researcher takes part in the study as if he too were attendees to the event.

This is also called "secret shoppers." Some of the main advantages of this are that the researcher gets the actual customer experience of the event and more than one "observer" at the event to get different views. Cleland says that the evaluation should be done during the entire life cycle of the project. There are four different stages that could be called evaluation stages. These are pre-project evaluation, where connection shows the objectives and overall strategy of the project. Ongoing project evaluation, states the measure of a project during its life cycle.

Project completion evaluation, as an immediate assessment of success upon the completion. Finally a post-project evaluation, a down-the-road assessment of the success of the project after the dust and confusion have settled should be done. Paul Stanley refers to the topic when to evaluate like this "We never tie a client's promotional success to the number of tickets sold. The programme focus should be on the three to four weeks prior to the event itself, on the weeks following the event and on actually paying the cost of the event."

The project team and the project owner have the responsibility for evaluating the project. The evaluation should be carried out as closely as possible to where and when the work has been done. A problem that can arise when an external researcher comes in and does the evaluation is that he/she interferes with a team that is not used to having someone watching over them. Also, the difference between free research and evaluation of projects is that the results of the project evaluation should be used directly and also that the evaluation is usually financed by the project.

Depending on who is doing the evaluation, the result might change. A qualitative result is built upon a trustworthy relationship between the researcher and the client. Important aspects to consider are: what should be monitored and evaluated, where and what should the monitoring and evaluation carry out, what monitoring tools should be used, and who should take care of the monitor and evaluate?

Image

Image is how the customer understands and looks upon the product, and a definition is "how the consumers experience the brand." An event can give the customer a clear picture of the corporate identity that the company is striving for. Usually the image consists of different key factors that the customer receives during different times and in different places. These key factors could be the communication that the organisation has the physical environment, products, service, ethics, social responsibility, engagement in social and local happenings, and the behaviour of representatives from the organisation.

The experience at the event may of course result in direct sales, but normally they help to build image and create positive associations around the brand that will lead to more sales later on. Image can create lots of competitive advantages compared to other brands. This is especially true when the differences between the brands are small. A positive image can lead to not only increased sales, but it can also strengthen the relationships with all interesting parties within and outside the organisation, facilitate new employment, increase the tolerance of customers, and facilitate crises. However, even though the main objective with the event is not to change or build image, there is always a possibility for the customer to change his/her opinion and image of the organisation.

A way to measure the Image that the event has created could be done by looking at their exposure rate. Hoyle talks about the possibility to evaluate an event's success by looking at the media exposure rate during the event. He believes that the value of an independently written article appears more credible to the reader than an advertisement does. He also says that the real value of editorial cover rate is triple that of paid advertisement. However before using and trying to get media attention to an event it requires a careful analysis of the purpose, benefits and to see if the media is available to deliver the appropriate message. There are many different organisations that are working with observing the media and can deliver the exact amount of times a name of a brand or product figured in the media.

Positioning

When a company has decided to use Event Marketing they need to understand how Event Marketing can change the perception of the product in the customers mind, and the positioning of the product. According to Kotler, it is extremely important to have a specific positioning in the customer's mind, due to the fact that if a similar product has the same positioning there is no need for the customer to buy your product. It is important to create an image and a correct positioning for customers that create differentiation between products.

The positioning distinguishes brands from each other and creates a place on the market and in the consumer's minds for a particular project. The idea behind positioning is to create brand awareness, which ideally leads to long-term brand loyalty. The positioning is a two-stage process, indicating which category the brand should be placed in, and the differences between the brands in this category. Products are becoming more and more alike. A company needs to diversify its product from competitors' products.

An organisation has three main perspectives for differentiation. They are: total perspective, more value for money, produce trustworthy products at a reasonable price, product perspective, offer a better product, that is newer, faster, cheaper, with unique selling attributes, and customer perspective, to know the customer better, and thereby reply to their needs faster. The last perspective, the customer perspective, involves the relationship between the customer and the organisation.

An event is the physical meeting between customer and organisation, and thereby Event Marketing can be used as a tool to build relationships and create differentiation. The idea behind positioning is to create brand awareness. Direct advantage of using Event Marketing is that it creates high brand awareness around the product. The value of the brand lies in the mind of the potential buyers, and not with the business itself. Branding is part of the marketing strategy and product differentiation.

The brand can communicate more directly with the consumer than the product itself can; if the brand is seen as having a personality and symbolising certain values. This is due to the fact that the brand has an emotional appeal to the consumers. A trend within Event Marketing is to involve more cultural aspects at events. According to Öqvist, the cultural aspects of events are not used extensively today. He further argues that culture and brand strategy go hand in hand. Over time, a relationship between the customer and the product can be developed into brand loyalty. This loyalty is characterised by a positive attitude towards the brand, and over time continued purchase of the same brand.

A company seeks high brand loyalty because it creates stability and provides an opportunity to gain high market share and profit. The development of brand loyalty can be seen as a three-step model. The first step is to create an interest for the product in the consumer. When time has past, the consumers will simplify their buying detour through the product and the connection between the brand and the target audience is strengthened. The third step is where brand recognition is created, which is important for creating the long-term brand loyalty.

One way to see if the positioning of a product is correct is to look at the directsale results. There are some other measurement tools that can be used when evaluating. One model is called the "Cost-Benefit-Analysis model" which can be used as an economic evaluation tool. By using this model, the costs are be measured against economic profit. The analysis can compare different alternatives. It is often used when comparing different ways to reach the same goal, and identify the less expensive alternative.

According to theory, to measure the awareness levels, or the attitude changes, there has to be a pre-event awareness or attitude knowledge of the customers. Attitudes or opinions are one of the simpler and most common ways of evaluation. This could be done with regular questionnaires. There are different models within attitude evaluations that could be used. The organisation needs to know what exactly they need to measure, the brand awareness, attitude change, or knowledge of product etc. Brand awareness and attitude change could be measured by a focus group prior to the event or during the event if there is a long-term commitment to it, and if the event is staged more than once.

During a Coca-Cola awareness event, the evaluators used questionnaires as one way of measuring the expectations of the performance compared to the actual performance. The differences between the two were referred to as disconfirmation. When it comes to measuring increased sales, the organisation can do this in many different ways. They should not only look at the exact sales of a product in a store, but rather try to see the link between the distribution and stores' sales etc. Also, the sales need to be compared with a specific time of the year, or geographical areas, etc.

13

Managing Festival Tourism for Sustainable Development

Tourism is considered of value in economic development for its considerable income generating properties and its ability to provide jobs. Despite this the benefits of tourism have been challenged as concern over tourism's wider negative impacts and the implications of these for sustainability have become more clearly understood. Moreover, sustainable tourism itself remains a contested concept. The tensions around sustainable tourism remain despite its promotion at the highest level, and what has been described as a 'rigid acceptance that the principles and objectives of sustainable development can easily be transposed onto most tourism development contexts'. In spite of the continuing vigorous debate it seems reasonable to suggest that a favourable symbiosis between certain types of tourism, such as festival tourism, and sustainable development may exist.

Festival tourism was termed 'an emerging giant' over 10 years ago but even now there appears to be a relatively small and disparate literature on the subject. Most frequently used as a 'catchall' term to include special event tourism and festivals of any size or organisational persuasion, festival tourism makes a complex topic of study that has been tackled from a variety of perspectives. Broadly speaking these may be grouped into four areas of interest: sociological; leisure participation; community development and from a tourism industry perspective.

Festivals can extend the tourist season, generate revenue for governments, and have 'positive economic impacts on the local economy' by generating income, supporting existing businesses and encouraging new start-ups. Mitchell and Wall's 1986 study found that smaller festivals produced most economic benefit but that as festivals became more established the economic impact became relatively less significant. They were researching the economic benefit in a relatively narrow sense, they suggest that a greater balance between economic and community benefit is desirable in countering local resistance to festival growth. They note '. . . the influx of additional tourists results in a change in community infrastructure to serve the needs of festival visitors' so that, as festivals grow and begin to make stronger links outside the locality, local entrepreneurs are likely to become 'resentful' and that consequently the economic benefits of the festival become less significant.

Illustrating this point, research on the economic impact of the internationally famous Brecon Jazz Festival reportedly confirms its income generating properties. However, almost simultaneously, reports of local businesses' growing dissatisfaction with the festival's 'impact on town life' over the festival period began to appear. News items on local businesses closing for the duration of festival and of local retailers' 'growing unhappiness' with its impact on their livelihood were reported in the run-up to the event.

Concern over the future of Brecon Jazz culminated in 2001 with the withdrawal of sponsorship by long-standing supporters Hyder Group and British Airways. In a similar vein, the world famous Glastonbury Festival was cancelled in 2001 reportedly due to concerns over exceeding the capacity of the site. The population of the Mendip region doubles during the festival and there were doubts about the ability of essential services (police, fire, hospitals) to cope in an emergency. Residents make regular complaints to Mendip Council regarding the invasion of visitors to the area and concerns over the safety of festival-goers include the potential for mass dehydration and food poisoning. Such reports surrounding apparently 'successful' and 'internationally acclaimed' festivals must be a cause for concern to organisers everywhere.

Though economic impact studies continue to suggest that festival tourism can benefit local tourism-related businesses income generation alone is not enough. If festival tourism is to contribute to sustainable localities it is reasonable to suggest that a spread of benefits for residents and business should be sought. For communities living on marginal incomes, being able to pay for a college education on car parking fees or being able to raise $14,000 in 10 days by selling fudge is 'too significant to be ignored'.

An hypothetical 'social multiplier' has been developed to explain the ways in which festival tourism contributes to increased 'organisational activity' in a locality bringing improved leadership, improved local accountability, better public-private co-operation and the investment of profits back into the community. Festivals are often intimately related to the maintenance and celebration of community values and ultimately, to their survival. Local festivals are said to be celebrations of community and effectively to serve as a public demonstration of 'what a community is all about'. It is also argued that although few rural festivals are about 'money-making' many play an important role in generating a visitor industry for their host communities.

Visitors to rural festivals are often from urban centres and bring economic benefits to local shops, restaurants, hoteliers, craft producers, entertainers and all manner of goods and service providers in the festival area. Such festivals are considered a success if they provide 'wholesome fun' and cover expenses, but they are also meant to: raise funds for service organisations, put money in the pockets of local vendors, provide a showcase for local talent, create a positive image of the host community, instil community pride, promote clean-ups and fix-ups and make business sponsors happy.

In a similar vein and in the context of the 'blossoming' of festivals in rural America, it is claimed that festivals attract tourists who might otherwise never visit and that: as a delightful bonus, the beneficial side effects of festivals extend well beyond generating tourism dollars and include strengthening rural communities and enriching the quality of small town life. In addition to the social positives it is also notable that examples of environmental improvements may be found at festival locations.

As festival time approaches, residents will become involved in activities that make the locality more presentable. Over time, motivation and money is generated for community improvement projects such as 'redeveloping downtowns, preserving and restoring historic buildings, renovating old theatres, constructing parks and community centres, planting trees, paving streets and installing holiday decorations'.

While environmental negatives may occur from a transport perspective, an advantage of festivals is that they are temporarily-short lived and, with effective planning, are unlikely to pose the problems for the community that 'year round' tourists might. This link between tourism and environmental preservation and conservation has long been recognised. There is some evidence to suggest that festival tourism, with its links to community development and concern for local environments, could be said to be one of the most sustainable forms of tourism development, as its very nature demands a balanced approach.

Economic Growth and Sustainability

Early attempts to measure development concentrated on economic growth demonstrated as rate of change of GDP per head, but in recent years there has been a trend toward a greater consideration of socio-economic and environmental variables. This has often been encapsulated within the elusive term 'quality of life'. While current notions of development usually incorporate economic growth they are not necessarily the same thing. Economic growth can occur simultaneously with increases in poverty, unemployment and inequality. Therefore it is argued that development is concerned with the human betterment that may be achieved by improvements in lifestyles and opportunities.

Eisenschitz and Gough have traced the burgeoning of local economic development activities in western economies and note the commonality between them: . . . across this variety there is a widely shared framework: the need for local control of the economy, the use of indigenous resources, the promotion of enterprise and the mobilisation of community co-operation. These are seen as key to the health or revival of local economies, and indeed as important means to national economic regeneration. Arguably, despite the variety, three distinct approaches to local economic development can still be identified: 'conventional economic development', 'community economic development', and 'sustainable economic development'.

The conventional approach emphasises policies which operate within the formal economy through such measures as inward investment and promotion, the building and management of industrial workspaces, assisting new sectors of growth and supporting training schemes. Community economic development focuses on the interface between the informal and formal economies and promotes the 'well-being' of the community it serves. The latter approach can be either complementary to the conventional approach or an alternative to it.

'More sustainable' forms of local economic development involve consideration of the 'longer term' and 'inter-generational equity'. Notions of 'carrying capacity' and 'balance' (social, economic and environmental) are common, fostering participation and community ownership of initiatives. These acknowledge the need for a shift in the way localities operate and imply a need for changes in lifestyles.

Sustainable local economic development is not, as yet, a checklist of activities or policies to be 'ticked off' when achieved, but the work is ongoing. An example would be the attempts being made to develop frameworks which allow local authorities or other responsible bodies to audit and review their progress towards the implementation of sustainable tourism.

New ways of thinking about the sustainability continuum are developing and there is some evidence of a convergence of ideas around sustainable approaches to local economic development that makes links to all aspects of a locality. As awareness of the concept of sustainable local economic development has increased, there is a recognition that economic growth alone is 'not enough'. Despite such high level support for the concept there remains less agreement on how it might be achieved.

Many organisations (public, private, voluntary and cross-sector partnerships) are actively seeking ways to implement sustainable forms of development at the local level. One such is the charity Forum for the Future which seeks to find ways to 'improve the lot' of local economies.

This organisation works to push forward the boundaries of understanding by taking a 'positive, solutions oriented approach' to sustainable development.

In 1998 Forum for the Future produced an 'Agenda for Sustainable Local Economic Development' which, when set within a policy framework, provides an initial step towards establishing what sustainable local economic development might actually look like. Its core themes (Table 1) represent key elements of a model of sustainable local economic development that seeks to combine satisfying work, wealth creation, social inclusion and a healthy environment. The activities set out as following from the core themes are seen as essential for the development of a sustainable local economy.

Table 1 Agenda for sustainable local economic development

1. *Capacity Building and Training* – providing a platform to tackle social exclusion and ensure that people are able to make the most of available opportunities.
2. *Community Enterprise* – including support for institutions that promote sustainable community regeneration, and encouragement for social entrepreneurs, community businesses and co-operatives which generate jobs and income and meet wider social and environmental objectives.
3. *Access to Credit and Capital* – mechanisms that provide access to, and control of, low cost credit and capital should be fostered for individuals, businesses and community enterprises.
4. *Local Business Development* – a supportive framework can assist the creation of new businesses and help local firms to grow and prosper. This includes existing business support agencies, and making the most of new business opportunities such as in the cultural and environmental sectors.
5. *Sustainable Approaches to Inward Investment* – a selective approach is needed which considers all the impacts of a development and related infrastructure. Only those proposals that have positive impacts on the local

community, businesses and the environment should be actively promoted.

6. *Responsible Business Practice* – promoting responsible business practice in terms of good environmental management, valuing employees and developing links with local communities. This should be viewed as part and parcel of work to support the survival and growth of businesses.
7. *Access to and Distribution of Work* – can be improved through good childcare and public transport provision, as well as mechanisms like local labour schemes which match employers' needs with local skills, and Intermediate Labour Markets that offer paid work experience and meet community needs.
8. *Trading Locally* – Supply chains between local firms can benefit businesses and the environment, and making the most of local resources can create jobs and reduce 'leakage' of skills and wealth from an area. Local currency systems can also encourage people to better value, develop and use their skills.

The framework identified by Forum for the Future (Local Agenda 21, lifelong education, promoting health, tackling poverty, environmental quality, sustainable infrastructure and building partnerships for change) are already stated objectives of most, if not all, local authorities in the UK. This means that, in principle, the framework for a policy of sustainable local economic development should already be in place, or at least in the process of being introduced in every locality.

Research Model on the Nature of Festival Tourism

The diverse and fragmented nature of festivals, and consequently of festival tourism, might have afforded a problem of construct validity for this study. However, the fact that not all types of festival were addressed in this research was not a problem for two reasons. Firstly, this study is dealing with an area of research that has, to the best of the authors' knowledge, not been addressed before and consequently any results will have a unique significance of their own. Secondly, a festival typology was developed for the purpose of this research to provide a framework for a multiple embedded case study approach. Three types of festival were identified: (i) 'home-grown'; (ii) 'tourist-tempter'; (iii) 'big-bang'.

A 'home-grown' festival is essentially small scale, bottom-up and run by one or more volunteers for the benefit of the locality. A 'tourist-tempter' festival is one that is aimed specifically at attracting visitors to stimulate local economic development. A 'big-bang' festival is essentially a marketing tool that promotes a myriad of related activities over a defined geographical area.

Three cases, all sharing the 'arts, culture and entertainment' theme, were identified for study as typical examples of the defined festival typologies. These festivals were spatially accessible (within the South Wales area), intended to generate festival tourism (were not just for local people) and, crucially, were run by organisations willing to be involved in the project. At each case study site a 'festival organiser' (FO) was identified and was the subject of a semi-structured interview. The FO interviews were face-to-face and an average of 90 minutes long.

Snowballing led to follow-up interviews being undertaken with a variety of significant actors including local authority project officers and business and voluntary sector festival contributors. Follow-up interviews were largely undertaken by telephone and lasted between 20 and 30 minutes. Corroborative interviews used primarily to confirm information were shorter, more structured and conducted by telephone (in one case by e-mail). Each case studied was the subject of between five and seven interviews comprising a core interview with the FO, semi-structured interviews and corroborative interviews.

A variety of secondary sources (economic development strategies and action plans, tourism strategies, festival brochures, funding applications and project summaries) were used to assess the validity of claims made by interviewees and to provide context. Interviews were transcribed within 24 hours and where a tape recorder was not used, transcriptions were returned to interviewees for verification. Questions asked were based entirely on the eight Forum for the Future themes set out in Table 1, but respondents were allowed to develop their answers more widely.

An history or 'context' of each festival was elicited at the start of the FO interview. Occasionally it was necessary to interpret some of the language of the themes for the interviewees. For example, festival volunteers were not expected to be familiar with terms such as 'capacity building'. The usual limitations of qualitative interviews must, of course, apply. The results of the case studies can not, and have not been, 'pooled'. Instead, this methodology follows a replication logic (producing different results for predictable reasons), rather than a sampling one.

The divergent nature of the cases studied mean that each site could not be researched using a rigidly identical format. The very nature of the subject matter denies a sampling approach, as no two festivals could ever be identical in nature. The general analytic strategy was to transfer the outcomes of the interviews to a gridmatrix allowing for an immediate impression of the pattern match between the picture of sustainable local economic development and the festival being studied. In order to reach the conclusions necessary to complete the gridmatrix an element of judgement was necessary. The study is strengthened by the use of the Forum for the Future themes as its theoretical proposition allowing for a pattern-matching logic.

The 'home-grown' festival example is based on a small market town in the County of Monmouth with a population of around 10,000 inhabitants of which an above average proportion (for Wales) is economically active. Employment in agriculture has reduced in recent years while the tourism sector (largely hotels and catering) is increasing and is expected to grow by 7% in the next two years.

Despite a relatively healthy economy a recent report undertaken for the county's economic development strategy highlighted that high economic activity masks a problem of low wages, with many household incomes at less than £10,000.

The festival aims to 'provide two weeks of summer entertainment and fun for people of all ages including residents of the town, people from surrounding localities and for the many visitors to the area'. The festival has operated for the last eight years and includes a variety of music, literature, storytelling, poetry, theatre, painting, crafts and dance events.

Funding for the festival comes from a variety of public sector grants, donations, sponsorship and ticket sales. The festival is organised by a key volunteer, a supporting committee from the local Tourist Association and there is no profit motive. The precise festival location has been protected at the request of the FO.

The 'tourist-tempter' festival takes place in the post-industrial town of Caerphilly. The Unitary Authority has followed a policy of 'pump priming' to encourage tourism, while its economic development strategy declares its commitment to sustainable tourism development. The festival began on a relatively small scale in 1998, obtained grant funding from the European Regional Development Fund in its second year and has grown in scale and scope. It runs from Friday to Sunday at the end of July and is sponsored by local businesses and organisations both public and private. The festival aims to recreate a 19th century food market with games, street entertainment, theatre and crafts. Evening music events, a funfair and comedy entertainment add a more up-to-date element.

The festival was organised primarily by the local council's tourism officer. It does not seek to make a profit and is effectively part of a larger strategy to promote the area, building on its main tourist attraction (its castle) and the nationally recognised food product, Caerphilly Cheese. The 'big-bang' festival considers the case of Swansea. The festival initiative was in effect a newly created marketing campaign designed to promote the plethora of events (over 65) which occur in the area between April and August.

Over two-thirds of the events were promoted by the Council, while other contributors included a national charity activity event, intercultural arts events driven from other parts of the principality and various local groups and businesses which have become partners in the festival project. Here the term 'festival' is used to promote an image of the destination as being a vibrant place to visit with more than just natural assets to offer visitors. In this case a full-time festival organiser was employed with the assistance of grant aid. This type of festival is, by its very nature, somewhat different to the traditional definition of a festival as a 'celebration of local values and distinctiveness' but, clearly, the nature of festivals is dynamic.

Research Process and Results

The results obtained for each case study site are summarised as follows. It clearly demonstrates the extent to which each of the three cases stimulate activities that fall within the sustainable local economic development themes as described in the Forum for the Future agenda.

Theme 1: Capacity building and training

As discussed earlier, festivals have the potential to provide opportunities for community development, yet in only one of these cases (the 'tourist-tempter') did the festival appear to be making a recognisable contribution in this area. Here local people were able to gain formal training in crowd control via an accredited course at a local further education college, which also exempted entrants from stage one of an National Vocational Qualification (NVQ) programme.

The festival had also encouraged and supported the creation of a Youth Theatre group that allowed young people to begin training as theatre technicians. Some local voluntary groups also used the festival as a forum for interacting with the wider public to raise awareness of social issues such as deafness, social intolerance and the value of voluntary work.

In contrast, the 'home-grown' festival yielded only minor, informal opportunity for community involvement, with no evidence of formal training opportunities. With the 'big-bang' festival example it may be conceivable that some opportunities for capacity building and training might have been available, but this could not be confirmed by any of the six interviewees.

Theme 2: Access to credit and capital

None of the cases studied indicated positive activity arising from the festival in terms of facilitating access to credit and/or capital for locals. The 'home-grown' festival surpluses, generally less than £2000, were used as a float to cover expenses from one year to the next. The 'big-bang' festival had no discernible links to mechanisms that provide access to, and control of, low cost credit and capital. In the case of the 'tourist-tempter' festival, the FO did not have any links to social investment or 'micro finance' schemes that aim to help community enterprises and business ventures get off the ground, and was unaware that three credit unions were already operating in the area.

Theme 3: Community enterprise

Some evidence of indirect activity in this area was found at the 'tourist-tempter' festival. Some voluntary and self-help groups took stalls at the festival at a reduced rate and used it to raise awareness of social issues, to generate funds and to attract new supporters for their activities in the locality. However, none of the festivals appeared to support institutions such as *Development Trusts* that promote sustainable regeneration and engender the participation of local people in improving their communities. Similarly the research did not uncover examples of direct festival involvement in the encouragement of social entrepreneurs, community businesses, or enterprises and co-operatives which generate jobs, income and meet wider social and environmental objectives.

Theme 4: Local business development

In all three cases there were indications that the festivals, at least indirectly, were helping some local firms grow and prosper. The 'home-grown' festival FO stated 'the festival is about supporting existing businesses not about creating more', indicating that wealth creation is a consideration of the festival but that any wealth generation is likely to be limited to an existing, relatively small, business elite. At this site a group of local craft workers who had created a workshop space in a renovated barn held an 'open day' during the festival to encourage visitors to their centre and so increase business. However, there was little evidence of new business trading purely as a result of the festival.

When asked about local business development, the 'tourist-tempter' festival FO claimed that the festival had encouraged the reintroduction of production of a local, nationally recognised cheese and the sponsorship of the annual 'race' (a key part of the festival) by the food producing firm. However, the local manager of the food firm in question saw the reintroduction of the product simply as a result of 'local demand for it to be made in the town again'.

The FO reported that national non-departmental government bodies involved in supporting business in the principality had become involved with food producers in the area through the medium of the festival. For the 'big-bang' festival it was clear that, while it had the capacity to aid business prosperity in general, there was concern within at least one firm that the festival was actually damaging a commercial leisure business by directing visitors to free public events. One respondent, when asked about the impact on local business development, commented '. . . you could argue that the Festival was good for the city but I'm not entirely convinced that it was money well spent. I think it was more about the Council events department saving money on their own publicity than anything else'. On the other hand, another respondent said 'we've really been over the moon with the whole thing and it didn't cost us anything. I've been meaning to call someone to thank them . . . . I must do that very soon'. This illustrates the conflicting claims made by interviewees.

Theme 5: Sustainable approaches to inward investment

All the festivals studied indicated a positive response on this issue. In the case of the 'home-grown' festival a 'most-local' approach is taken, while at the 'tourist-tempter' festival a small local ice-cream producer has sole rights to trade at the festival despite interest from bigger, non-local suppliers. For the 'big-bang' festival it is a requirement of the ERDF funding and of the Council's own Best Value policy that local suppliers be used. However, a Council representative suggested that this requirement caused them some difficulty in its application due a lack of suitable suppliers in the area.

Theme 6: Responsible business practice

There was no clear evidence of either the 'big bang' or the 'home-grown' festivals contributing under this theme. Indeed the FO of the latter stated: 'we would not interfere with the way people do business'. At the 'tourist-tempter' festival health and safety issues were paramount and non-government departmental bodies had recently become involved in helping festival exhibitors raise levels of food safety and hygiene.

Quality control of craft production had been considered by the festival organisers, while fun-fair ride owners had been required to use Council electricity generators that were cleaner, quieter, and generally less polluting than those they would normally use. There was evidence of the encouragement of public transport use for the festival in which the Agenda 21 officer had been involved, although the latter expressed concern over the lack of attention being paid to recycling linked to the festival.

Theme 7: Access to and distribution of work

There was little or no evidence of a sustained positive impact on job creation from any of the festivals studied. While it could be argued that existing jobs are generally supported by 'home-grown' festival activity there was no direct evidence of a significant contribution here. Similarly, in the case of the 'big-bang' festival, though contributing events may provide some form of work there was no formalised policy regarding its access or distribution.

At the 'tourist-tempter' festival steward posts were created but direct job creation was not seen as a high priority due to the festival's temporary nature. In addition, although the FO was keen to relate anecdotal evidence of jobs being supported by the festival, job creation was 'played down' by several local companies when this issue was raised. Nevertheless, the same respondents conceded that the festival was generally a positive influence.

Theme 8: Trading locally

Low levels of business involvement in the 'home-grown' festival meant that there was no evidence of local firms working together in relation to the festival and no evidence of local currency systems operating in the area. Similarly, in the case of the 'big-bang' festival nothing could be identified which pointed to the festival promoting networking or encouraging local trade.

In the case of the 'tourist-tempter' festival there was some suggestion of limited networking between groups attending satellite meetings and the encouragement of non-departmental government bodies with the ability to support local businesses. One respondent did express concern that local charity groups were not given priority over national charities in accessing fund raising opportunities offered by the festival.

14

Impacts of Sporting Events on Host Communities

Hallmark events have been defined by Richie, "Major one time or recurring events of limited duration, developed primarily to enhance the awareness, appeal and profitability of a tourism destination in the short/or long term. Such events rely for their success on uniqueness, status, or timely significance to create interest and attract attention."

Some literature focuses on the primary function of the hallmark tourist event as being an opportunity for an area to "put itself on the map" and therefore draw tourists to the area for economic gain. Some argue that the hallmark event may be something pursued by and for the exclusive benefit of the local business community, rather for the broader community. Whether this be in the local, state or national level, increasingly of importance, is the media coverage of major sporting events. Whether an event is community based and/or driven, or promoted by the business community or a corporate entity for financial gain, all rely on some form of media exposure for the area, which may attract attention for a short period or in some cases, over an extended term.

Impacts of Hallmark Events

There are six types of impacts that need to be addressed for particular hallmark events, they are economic, tourism/ commercial, physical, socio-cultural, psychological, and political. "There is a need to go beyond the glamour of hallmark events, and the supposed economically beneficial effects of such events, and subject them to rigorous interrogated economic, environmental, social and political analysis. The task of the researcher should be to compare the image of the event with the reality. Why, for what, and for whom, are these events held? And in so doing come to a more complete understanding of the urban impact of hallmark events"

The event impacts on the local community which is not entirely involved in the organisation of the event. It is therefore the responsibility of the local authority in allowing the event to occur, to have a full understanding of local community expectations and the organisers goals and objectives of the event. In understanding both points of view the local Council can make an informed decision on whether to approve the event and what conditions should be established.

It seems inevitable that if the event is to continue annually, the local community should be able to influence and be involved in planning of the event. The event could therefore be managed to minimise the negative impact by having due regard to the local communities views, and using them as a framework focusing and enhancing on the positive attributes. The major sporting event could then be beneficial to both the organiser and the local community in most aspects.

Effective Planning

Throughout the world, there have been many hallmark events with a lack of planning. "the citizens of Montreal are still paying for the construction of the 1976 Olympic games stadium while the people of Perth, Western Australia are faced with finding events which can utilised the 1962 Commonwealth Games stadium at Perry Lakes. Hence, it can be seen that planning is an essential ingredient but not only for the short term success of the hallmark event itself, but also in realising the longer term benefits that can accrue to a community in the holding of such events." Most major events, which are located usually in cities, are developed for the purpose of generating tourism and economic benefits to either the organiser or the area. This has lead to an approach where the event is organised because it has to occur for predetermined reasons. However, in some cases there appears to be a demand for an event, which may not necessarily be for economic reasons, and this has lead to local governments having to determine how to deal with unexpected event proposals.

Increasing examples of how a local community are being requested to assess events at short notice are rave parties, festivals, large group meetings in small towns and major sporting events. Major sporting events maybe attracted to an area which normally does not experience large numbers of people, due to a particular quality or attribute specific to the locality. There is a need to be prepared for a major event. For example, the America's Cup may have been staged in Perth, not only for economic reasons but due to the occurrence of strong wind at certain times of the year, good sailing conditions and facilities. Like wise, Lancelin to the north of Perth, has good wind surfing conditions which attract the world's best for an annual event. Other places such as Manjimup attract some of Australia's best motor cross riders and even the world rally tour comes to Western Australia partly due to the abundance of demanding tracks throughout the country side. In the same way, the world surfing tour demands events in high quality surf locations such as Margaret River. It is therefore a foregone conclusion, that interest in staging events in Margaret River will be prevalent and this one of the main reasons why the Augusta-Margaret River Shire frequently receives event applications.

There are four critical issues identified in the hallmark event planning process stated by, Hall they are:

> "The development of methods of forecasting for hallmark events, the role and manner of public participation in the planning process, the relationship between government agencies in hosting of hallmark events, and the staging of subsidiary or ongoing events due to the conduct of the hallmark event."

> "Planning of a hallmark tourist event should be concerned with the anticipation and regulation of the impacts of the event on the host community, and the promotion of the associated development in a manner which maximises short and long term economic, environmental and social benefits. Hence an evaluation of hallmark events to focus not only on the immediate economic aspects of the event but also the wider implications within the community and its physical surroundings".

It has been noted that there has been little study on the negative impacts of hallmark events on the local community. A reason for this, is that usually the study is based around what a hallmark event can do for an area. However, some areas are faced with the pressure for a hallmark event which may not necessarily be desired by the community.

In fact, the event and the following exposure from it, particularly with world wide media distribution, could directly impact negatively on the community on a long term basis. The occurrence of one event in an area based on surfing for example in Margaret River, could expose the particularly high quality region for Surfing to a greater number of people. Therefore drawing larger numbers of tourists to the area to participate in the sport of surfing.

Although, this seems productive from a economic point of view, the local community may well be disadvantaged by the level of exposure. The reasons being, they live in that location to experience the high quality surf, and increased tourists may lesson their accessibility to that resource. At the same time, the environment in which they live, will be negatively impacted upon, as increased development pressure is likely to occur to meet the increased tourism demand. In turn the increased development pressure may contribute to higher land values and therefore generally impact on the local people socio-economically.

Therefore, it is important to ensure that staging of the event does not adversely impact on the local community and also that planning is undertaken to ensure that the long term impact created by increased attention the area, due to its exposure from the hallmark events, can be dealt with appropriately. The community in accepting increased exposure could be satisfied with the knowledge, that the pressure will be dealt with in a manner considered acceptable to them. This seems very relevant to Margaret River, Western Australia. For example, many people have moved to the area for its high quality environment, country living and lifestyle. It is therefore not a surprise when exposure of that area, which to many appears to be "hidden away", is not welcomed by some.

Hall says that "Hallmark events are commonly regarded by government and private industry as essential for the creation of tourism opportunities, employment, and increasing the prominence of the host community in the market place." And as Hall continues "The Commonwealths support for the Grand Prix acknowledged the unprecedented international exposure for Australia and significant economic benefits in areas of tourism, employment and business opportunities." State or national government and private industry tend to focus on economic and tourism benefits. There is an opportunity for local government to consider broad economic/tourism benefits with an appreciation of host community attitudes in mind.

Socially, most small towns in Western Australia have an existing social situation which is fairly stable and most people are content with that situation. This is reflected in many stable or non transient populations in country areas. However, hallmark events do have the potential to change and attract further attention to an area, which will eventually have a social impact due to the influx of tourists. If the influx of tourists during an event is accepted, it is sometimes because there is not a dramatic long term increase in visitors. This would be the case with the Dowerin Field Days. It would be unlikely that many people would visit Dowerin other than for the Hallmark Event. Future tourism is not expected by the host community.

In some areas, the influx of tourists will be seen by the local community as a positive thing. It may be welcomed. However, in other instances it will be seen as a negative influence and unless the negative impacts are managed and therefore reduced, the hallmark event will never be completely accepted by the local community which hosts it.

More recently there has been a shift towards consideration of the physical and social impacts. These are often typified as unquantifiable and negative - the ecological and social price for the economic benefit. Visitor management involves a trade off between these impacts."

Methods of Acquiring Information

There are two main methods of acquiring information are "Qualitative and Quantitative."

Qualitative

There are methods of :

— Surveys

— Delphi technique

— Judgment—aided model

Quantitative

There are methods of :

— Time series

— Gravity and trip generation model

— Multi variant aggression

Hosting of Hallmark Events

Hall indicates those determined by the

— To upgrade cultural activity in the community.

— To attract tourists.

— To involve the community in a civic celebration.

— To develop popular participation in arts, crafts, sports and athletics.

— To advance and promote the community for public benefit.

— To promote cultural and political exchange.

— To create or strength a spirit of goodwill between the community's social or ethnic groups.

— To promote the utilisation of tourist facilities in the off season.

— To call public attention to the unique characteristics or attractions of the community.

— To earn revenue that can be used to provide a needed but otherwise unattainable social benefit for the community.

It is recognised that objectives provide "a measure with which to assess the success of events and provide a focal point for co-ordination of the event organisational."

Site Considerations

Another factor considered important are site considerations such as :

— Facility design.

— Landuse.

— Site Planning.

— Accessibility.

— Security and

— Environmental constraints.

There is a need to form strategies which can be used to successfully manage the site and its characteristics. Recognise the attributes and limitations of the site.

A Case Study of Margaret River in Western Australia

The Margaret River Masters is a professional surfing event, run at beach known as "Surfer's Point" within the small town of Prevelly near Margaret River (275km south of Perth Western Australia). The event is currently organised by Surfing WA. Surfing WA is a government funded organisation established to manage and promote the sport of surfing within Western Australia.

The men's event has operated almost every year since 1985. In 1994, 1991 and 1988 the event was not held due to lack of sponsorship. In 1992, 1993, 1996 and 1997 a women's world tour event was also held. The event forms part of the world surfing tour organised by the Association of Surfing Professionals (ASP). The event is therefore in part, controlled by ASP Guidelines. A higher level of event under the ASP umbrella, requires higher amounts of prize money. Therefore, the organisers would be required to seek more sponsorship for a higher rated event. The world professional surfing tour is split into two categories, they are :

— The World Qualifying Series, (WQS) and

— The World Championship Tour (WCT).

The WQS is a series of events organised to give professional surfers the ability to qualify for the World Championship Tour. The top forty four surfers then surf in World Championship Tour Events to determine the world champion and other placings.

World Championship Tour Events have a higher rating and therefore require more prize money and sponsorship. All events are rated from 1 to 5 star events. A 5 star event would also provide the successful competitive surfer with more championship points. At the end of the year championship points are calculated to determine the world champion.

The Margaret River Masters is a World Qualifying Series Event which does attract some WCT Surfers and those other professional surfers aiming to score enough points to qualify for the World Championship Tour. The event is classified as a 4 star WQS Event and is required to be organised during the Australian leg of the world tour which is around February, March and April each year.

Surfing WA

Surfing WA is an organisation developed to oversee the

sport of surfing in Western Australia on behalf of the Australian Surfing Association. Surfing WA is funded by state and federal governments and other corporate sponsors.

Surfing WA is a non-profit organisation with the following mission statement:

> "Surfing WA is the states controlling body of Surfing in Western Australia and aims to provide continuous quality development and opportunity in surfing, relating to the areas of competition, environment, education and recreation."

In negotiating with the Shire of Augusta-Margaret River to conduct the Margaret River Masters, Surfing WA aim to promote competitive surfing in Western Australia. At the same time facilitate mental awareness and management practices, promote surfing as a recreational activity, and educate the community about the sport. The organisation not only organises the Margaret River Masters, but other various national, state and club events.

They also co-ordinate surfing coaching programmes throughout the state and coaches are required to be accredited with Surfing WA before operating any classes.

Surfing WA argue that organisation of the event is not for financial gain, but for the betterment of the sport of surfing in the four main areas outlined above.

Masters Event Location and Site Characteristics

The Margaret River Masters Event is held at "Surfers Point" at Prevelly Park near the mouth of the Margaret River. An area of land covering Reserve 41545 is leased to a local person for the purposes of operating the event annually and the lease is current until 1998. The site is accessed by one road only and is serviced by telephone and water from a soak nearby. Unfortunately, the area is not serviced with power, reticulated water and sewer facilities. As a result, event organisers have to take into account other methods of providing these services during the event.

The subject site is located on a steep sloped point or peninsula within the Leeuwin—Naturaliste Ridge system. The Leeuwin—Naturaliste Ridge contains various natural features including coastal bays and peninsulas. Much of the ridge is contained within the Leeuwin—Naturaliste National Park however, the subject site is located within an "A" Class Public Recreation Reserve vested with the Shire of Augusta-Margaret River. The ridge area is subject to high wind exposure from the north-west, west and south-west. The geology of the area is frequented by limestone over granite bedrock. The area is not common to occurrences of ground water and therefore supplies are limited.

Due to the high exposure to the weather and salt from the ocean, vegetation cover is poor and a high level of organic matter is built up within the top soil. The area is susceptible to wild fire due to heavy build up of fuel. Much of the land systems are comprised of coastal dunes and limestone outcrops which are experiencing weather erosion. Most of the land within the lease area for the Margaret River Masters is uncleared and typical of the Kilcarnup Dunes Land System. The indicates that there are a number of current development pressures on the area, one of which is recreation. "Similar to the Gracetown Ridge System, the Kilcarnup system is under considerable pressure from recreational pursuits involving access to the coast for swimming, surfing and fishing purposes. In Places, this has caused considerable environmental degradation."

Issues including accessibility, evacuation strategies, susceptibility to wild fire, fragile cliff sections or overhangs and lack of services and facilities all combine to make the area one which requires planning measures to be implemented during the event. These measures will therefore minimise the potential occurrence of related problems.

Conservation and Land Management Approaches

Discussions with the Department of Conservation and Land Management have revealed that in dealing with major sporting events in a coastal situation, a similar approach to that utilised by Council at present would be employed. The focus however, would be on assessing the particular site to be utilised, having regard for the infrastructure available and environmental characteristics.

Within the National Park Management Plan, there are guidelines for coastal use and this sets the framework under which CALM operates. A botanist is commonly used by CALM to ascertain locations of significant flora. Cliff risk and geological assessments are also undertaken. A rehabilitation specialist is utilised and staff are trained in rehabilitation techniques. Given the ongoing pressure from the community on the "Surfers Point" and "Rivermouth" areas, and the annual Margaret River Masters Surfing Event, it would be advantageous for Council to assess the site in more detail. This would involve, vegetation, geological, facility provision, fire risk and rehabilitation assessments.

The Surf Coast Shire in Victoria, have prepared a series of management reports for the Bells Beach Surfing and Recreation Reserve near Torquay. An erosion and drainage management report has also been compiled which identifies erosion areas, provides a landform description and recommendations for accessibility methods. The erosion report identifies major erosion sites and specifically identifies needs and methods of rehabilitating erosion areas.

The Surf Coast Shire Council, Victoria, have also contracted a geo-technical investigation for the purposes of assessing temporary grandstands. The erosion report investigates the proposed structures, the existing conditions, slope stability and recommendations for viewing platforms, TV camera decking and visitor boardwalks. This is also something that the Shire of Augusta-Margaret River should investigate for the "Surfers Point" area if the event is to continue in the future and grow in stature.

A proposal for the development of an environmental strategy for the professional surfing event held at Bells Beach in Victoria was prepared by Sane and the Surfrider Foundation. This proposal was aimed to establish a display and various activities during the event, to promote environmental awareness to visitors and competitors at the event. The aim being to encourage a philosophy of environmental awareness to those attending the event.

It is recommended that the Shire of Augusta-Margaret River investigate the preparation of an erosion and drainage management plan, a flora and fauna assessment plan, a geo-technical survey and an improved facility and infrastructure strategy for the Surfers Point area. This will enable not only a better strategy to be developed for the Margaret River Masters Professional Surfing Event but a strategy for management of the reserve for normal recreational use.

The survey conducted for this report, has identified that the Surfers Point and Rivermouth area are utilised by a high percentage of the local community on a regular basis. As a financial contribution, Council should contribute to the event through provision of such assessments.

Surfing Policy

Council developed a Surfing Policy to balance the

recreational and local user needs and to minimise damage and assist the recovery of coastal systems. Any organisation wishing to hold a contest on beaches and reserves under the control of Council, will be required to make an application in accordance with the provisions in the Policy. In December, 1996 a draft policy was adopted for the Cape to Cape Region, incorporating the Shire of Augusta-Margaret River, Conservation and Land Management (CALM) and Busselton Shire Council. This Policy incorporated the Shire of Augusta-Margaret River existing policy and included other issues considered relevant by CALM and the Busselton Shire. This was adopted in October 1997.

The Margaret River Masters event was incorporated into a section of the policy titled 'International Events'. The Policy states in part, that : "Only one International Event, organised in conjunction with Surfing WA, will be approved by Council in any one year. Confirmation shall be provided at least six months prior to the event date, in order to exclude other potential events. This confirmation is to be accompanied by an appropriate contribution. The Policy also stipulated standard conditions and locations considered acceptable for surfing events. The event is required to be assessed in accordance with this policy.

Approval for Professional Surfing Events

In addition to the Surfing Policy Council developed a set of standard conditions in a form of a booklet in March 1996. Council developed conditions to address the issues of concern considered important to control the event. The main issues are :

Carparking strategy

— The implementation of a carparking strategy included the provision of parking attendants, signage and the use of an area outside of the Prevelly townsite for most visitors to the event. This would achieve keeping persons out of the Prevelly townsite and therefore limiting impact on the local community.

- A carparking pass system was used so that visitors to the site who were involved in the event or needed to get to the event site, could be given a particular pass. Those passes included staff, media, competitors, VIP's etc. Residents to the Prevelly area were allowed to go through a checkpoint near the carparking area outside of town.
- A shuttle bus was used to transfer persons from the parking area to the event site.
- At least 20 parking attendants were required to implement the strategy. They were required to wear a uniform that was easily identifiable to the general public.
- The West Australian Police Department were required to be contacted for alterations to traffic movements in and around Prevelly and specific road closures were required to be approved by Council and applied for by the event organiser.

Crowd control

- Appropriate security and crowd control arrangements were required to be undertaken by the organiser to ensure fragile environmental areas were protected.
- Compliance was also required with regard to public safety and health requirements.

Environmental control

- The organiser was responsible for the provision of personnel to ensure that litter is controlled. In order to alleviate the demands on the organisers and enable manpower to be employed for environmental control, it was suggested that the organiser employ a local service group or sporting club to handle this aspect of the event. Council also assisted in the clean up after the event and provided rubbish bags and bins. At the completion of each day all rubbish was to be removed from the site by the organiser.

— Bush fire control methods were required to be implemented including the provision of a water tanker for emergency water supply and agreements with the local fire brigades in writing for necessary assistance prior to the event commencing.

— On the approved event plan environmental no-go areas were identified. Sensitive areas had been difficult to manage and it was decided that "Paraweb" fencing and taping was to be implemented to protect environmentally sensitive areas.

— It was also the responsibility of the organiser, to ensure that taping and fencing was maintained throughout the event and environmental areas patrolled by staff.

— It was also decided to implement signage and taping on the Friday morning of the event as it was not required in the first two to three days due to the lack of crowds. This would ensure that all fencing and taping had not been damaged or blown away before it was required.

Special infrastructure

A plan indicating where all infrastructure was to be located was developed in consultation with the organisers, the community and Council through a committee process. The infrastructure required for the event and indicated on the plan is as follows :

— A designated location for a helipad was required in the event that television coverage via helicopter was required. The relevant television stations were contacted prior to the event and provided with a location plan of the helipad and requested to comply with CAA standards.

— All buildings were required to comply with building by-laws to be checked by Council's Building Surveyor. In particular care was taken with regard to star pickets for public safety reasons, and location of tents and structures close to cliff edges.

— An electrical engineers certificate was also required seven (7) working days prior to the event.

— On occasion building fixtures penetrated the car park. The organiser was required to plug and repair any impacts on the carpark following removal of structures.

— Use of sound amplification equipment was to be confined to certain times of the day and was not to produce a volume of sound other than is reasonably necessary for the hearing and enjoyment of persons at the event. Location of sound amplification equipment was limited to designated locations. Only two speaker systems were allowed to be located in the fragile cliff system.

— All infrastructure including VIP tents and structures, media huts, judging equipment, food vendors and grand stands were required to be located in accordance with an approved plan.

Legal Documents and Approvals

The organiser was required to provide a varied assortment of licenses, approvals and agreements. This was to ensure that the event was considered acceptable to other authorities and legal and financial issues were addressed. The documents required were as follows:

— Department of Transport approval was required for the event. Any activity in the ocean, close to Surfers Point is under the jurisdiction of this authority.

— A lease agreement between Council and the organiser had been drawn up. This lease agreement gave Council a method of ensuring the organiser complied with conditions, reflected in the standard conditions booklet. As Surfing WA did not hold the current lease they had to provide written proof of transfer of that license into the organisers name prior to the event.

— The organiser had to provide Council with appropriate information indicating public liability and professional indemnity insurance.

— A license fee of $1,000 per day was charged by Council and payment of this was required at least two weeks prior to the commencement of the event.

— Alcohol was proposed to be served within the VIP area and an appropriate license holder was required to provide documentation indicating a liquor license was currently held.

— Under Health Act Regulations public building application forms were required to be completed.

Emergency Issues

An evacuation plan was required to be prepared by the organiser. All staff working at the event were required to have knowledge of this evacuation plan. Although simple, the plan indicated that all persons were to be directed to the beach via the stairwells. The most anticipated emergency was that of a bush fire.

— Ambulance and Sea Search and Rescue were designated locations at Surfers Point. Emergency Sea

Search and Rescue were briefed on methods of entering and exiting the water and rescuing any competitors from dangerous seas. Ambulance officers were located at the top of the stairwell and the stairwell was required to be kept clear at all times in case of an emergency.

— Loud speakers announcements were made to ensure that all persons were aware of ambulance and first aid facilities.

— As indicated earlier arrangements were made with the local bush fire brigade to ensure in the case of a fire, the equipment was placed on stand-by.

Advertising

To ensure that the public were aware of the event, the organisers were required to prepare a programme for the event. The programme was to be lodged with the Council and to be advertised in the local newspaper at least one week prior to the event. Any advertising of the event was also to indicate parking strategy issues and controls.

Signage

— All signage was required to be approved by Council.

— Signs were indicated on the infrastructure plan to provide necessary information to visitors to the event including where to park, where are the restricted areas, entry fees, and other controls examples, no dogs and no alcohol to be brought into the event site.

— Signs indicating when to slow down, required speed limits and environmentally sensitive areas were also identified.

— Signs in the townsite of Margaret River also provided information to visitors to the event.

Miscellaneous Issues

Other issues are as follows :

— Performance of the event was to be monitored by Council with a view to other events being approved in the future.

— An area was to be set aside close to the event site for recreational surfers to utilise other surfing breaks or areas within the lease area.

— A bus stop tent was to be located in a road reserve close to the event as a drop off location for spectators being transferred to the event site from outside of the area.

— Special permission was granted for Saturday evening activities at the event site, including the consumption of alcohol.

— Council made agreements to undertake the following works:

— pump out all toilets on site. (numbers are determined by the expected number of visitors to the event site)

— provide adequate rubbish bins and bags for the event.

— collect and remove on a daily basis all rubbish from the event site.

— provide all no parking signs for the event to be rented out to the organiser.

— assist the organiser in the clean up of the site by removing consolidated rubbish.

— provide Ranger Services over the weekend event

The organiser was required to provide all other infrastructure and equipment required for the event.

Statutory Approval for the Event

The Margaret River Masters is controlled by the Shire of

Augusta-Margaret River using four (4) mechanisms as follows:

Lease agreement

In accordance with the Land Act, Council has the vesting of the reserve where the event is held. The reserve is vested in the local authority for the purposes of "Recreation". The Department of Land Administration have also indicated that the vesting of the reserve also grants Council power to lease. Under this authority, the Council has developed a lease agreement which stipulates conditions under which the event must be managed and operated. Furthermore, this gives the Council the power to charge a fee, and set a time period for the lease.

Planning approval

Under Council's District Town Planning Scheme No. 11, which covers the subject site, Council can consider granting planning consent for the event as it is classified as development under the Town Planning and Development Act 1928 (as amended). The erection of structures, tents etc. is considered to be development and exclusive use of the area warrants application for planning approval. As a result, Council can stipulate special conditions annually, as part of any development/use approval issued for the event. This is considered important as from year to year variations to the event application occur. The Shire of Augusta-Margaret River have developed standard approval conditions for professional surfing events.

Permit To Undertake Activity on Council Reserve

The Shire of Augusta-Margaret River has a local law relating to parks, reserves and foreshores, which states in part that:

— "No person shall organise, arrange or take part in any function or activity on a reserve or foreshore unless a permit to hold or organise that function has been granted by the Council or the lessee of the Ground."

— "The Council may grant a permit to a person to hold a function or activity on a reserve or foreshore subject to such conditions as it sees fit. Such permits shall be in the form of Schedule Form No. 2".

— This local law defines the term function as including "any concert, fate, show, exhibition, gymcarna, sport, match or test between opposing teams in any game or single social gathering consisting of more than 20 persons."

Other provisions also apply in the local law. However, it is apparent that a lease could override the need to issue a permit for the Margaret River Masters Surfing event. However, this local law provides Council with another avenue in which to issue approval and control operations of an international surfing event.

15

Risk Management

Meetings and events are businesses; in fact, even a family event such as a wedding, christening, or bar mitzvah is a business. Events employ hundreds of people and involve large amounts of money. Event-goers pay money to attend these events, stay in hotels, and eat in public places. People are served by staff that have access to rooms, prepare food, or handle vast amounts of goods at shows. Within this system, then, there are numerous risks. The event cannot afford to have merchandise lifted, to have guests assaulted, or to have money stolen.

Not only are events open to risks by staff members, but they also attract large numbers of secondary people. Among these are vendors, restaurants, gas stations and transportation providers, places of lodging, and local store owners. These people are not directly linked to the event, but earn their living due to the event. Indeed, the larger the event, the more likely that it will cause spin-off economic opportunities. All of these factors carry two risks: (1) the risk of a negative occurrence both on site and off site and (2) the negative publicity that comes from this negative occurrence.

For example, let us look at a simple event, the family wedding. Weddings ought to be both simple and almost risk free. From a theoretical perspective, everyone shares a common joy, people are either family or friends of the bride and groom, and we suppose that from the caterer to the couple all want the same outcome. Yet, anyone who has ever attended a wedding knows that it is filled with risks. From the two families fighting, to the caterer serving the wrong food, to paint on chairs, to the loss of a wedding license, there is barely a wedding that occurs without some risk and some crisis.

As an event professional, it is important that you understand that it is significantly less expensive to manage a risk prior to the event than to deal with the crisis after it has occurred. Note also that in the world of events and meetings, safety and security issues often merge. Both safety and security are issues that must concern the event risk manager. In today's world of instant biochemical threats, it is dangerous not to view safety and security as two sides of the same coin.

Theoretical Principles of Risk Management

1. Events and meetings are a form of tourism and thus suffer from the same sociological phenomena as tourism.
2. Events and meetings often follow the same patterns, be they mega-events, such as an Olympic Games, or mini-events.
3. Whenever an act of violence occurs within the world of events or meetings, the media are almost certain to report it, forcing the local event industry to be embroiled in acts of crisis management.
4. Perceptions about an event crisis tend to be almost as devastating as the crisis itself.
5. The farther away one is from a crisis location, the worse the crisis will appear to be and the longer the crisis will remain in the collective travel subconscious.

These basic theoretical principles form the foundation for why risk management is so important to every aspect of the tourism industry from attractions to events, from hotels to meetings. Figure 1 gives you some idea of how interlocked the events and meetings part of the tourism industry is.

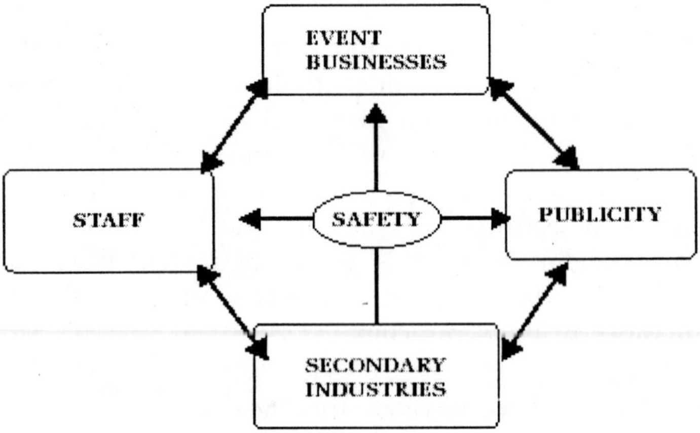

Figure 1.Comfort Zones of Event Stakeholders

According to the Travel Industry Association and the World Tourism Organisation, in the coming decades event managers can expect to see greater numbers of people travelling to concerts, conventions, meetings, and sports activities. The growth of the leisure industry will increase risk, and the need to manage that risk is becoming an ever-greater challenge to the entire tourism/leisure industry. Before we can even begin to examine some of the issues in managing risk, it is essential to review how leisure time is changing in the United States. Over the last decade, scholars have noted that leisure time has taken on the following characteristics:

— Shorter vacation periods

— Competition determined not by distance but by cost of travel to destination
— Greater access to information due to the Internet and the World Wide Web
— Greater exchange of "word of mouth" information between people who have never met each other
— New opportunities for cybercriminals

Throughout the world, both in developed and in emerging nations, risk managers in tourism and travel, and meetings and events must face and seek ways to confront crises prior to their occurrence. Risks to the events and tourism industries may come in many forms. Some of these risks are due to issues of potential violence, health and safety concerns, or unique and unexpected weather events such as floods, droughts, and hurricanes/typhoons.

Postmodern tourism is often driven by events and therefore the industry must improve its risk management practices to destroy this potential disease. The current period seems to be prone to great sociological mood swings. What may be seen as a risk or a crisis in one year may be ignored by the media in another year. The age of instant communication via satellite television and computers means that there is now selective knowledge and ignorance. Never have individuals around the world had greater access to information and never has there been greater levels of "information overload." What this plethora of information means is that we now have more information on how to handle risks and to prevent crises, and that the consequences of failure can be more devastating than ever before.

Historically oriented sociologists have observed the similarities that link the end of the nineteenth century to the end of the twentieth century. Event risk managers, then, must work in a world that can be very confusing as well as trying. Some of the major differences between life at the end of the nineteenth century and life at the end of the twentieth century indicate that we not only classify leisure in different ways, but that the risks involved in the pursuit of leisure have changed. Leisure is no longer viewed as simply idle time for the rich. Indeed, a simple list of some of the ways that we spend our leisure time would surprise our grandparents and great-grandparents. Following is a list of some of the events that occupy our time:

— Family and human life cycle events, such as weddings, family reunions, and barbecues
— Community events, such as school picnics, business outings, and holiday celebrations
— Organised shopping exhibitions
— Civil and political events
— Business meetings and conferences
— Sports events
— Concerts
— Religious gatherings and pilgrimages
— Local and national political gatherings
— Fairs and festivals

The preceding list demonstrates one of the major problems of risk management in the meetings and events industry. In the modern world, there is a great deal of spillover from a leisure activity to a business activity. Classical nineteenth-century authors of leisure such as Veblen enjoyed clear distinctions between leisure and work. In the twenty-first century, these distinctions no longer exist. Certainly all of the risks that are inherent in the other four entities mentioned are also part of the hajj. From the moment the traveller sets out for Mecca, he or she is subject to risk, be it in the form of clean water, sleeping facilities, safe travel, or crowd control. This spillover from one field to another is called "dedifferentiation."

In today's modern world, it is hard to dedifferentiate between what was once a simple family gathering and what is today a small convention. Today's mobile society has a very different view of leisure from that of past societies. "Leisure for them [us] closely resembles work, since much of it consists of strenuous and for the most part solitary exercise. Even shopping, their ruling passion, takes on the character of a grueling ordeal: 'Shop till you drop!' ". This dedifferentiation between work and play, as exemplified by the shop/drop syndrome, is one of the theoretical underpinnings to the understanding of risk management.

The onset of the information age in the twentieth century has closely paralleled the growth of the travel and tourism industry. Mass tourism is a phenomenon of the twentieth century. It was only with the end of World War II that travel, like so many products, entered the modern world of mass production. This success story also contains within it the seeds of crises. With millions of people travelling daily, and with the onset of the information age, word-of-mouth/computer information spreads rapidly, diseases are carried from one nation to the next, and the potential for violent cross-fertilisation, both in ideas and actions, becomes ubiquitous.

For example, throughout the world, tourists have been inundated with accounts of widespread acts of violence: in schools, in the workplace, and on public highways. The spread of information, both in written and in pictorial form, has never been so ever present. For example, television and radio broadcast events as they unfold, and the Web permits word-of-mouth dialogue in computerised form to spread instantaneously. Furthermore, the use of e-mail has transformed the world into an electronic village. All this rapid interchange among people makes the life of the event risk manager even more difficult as even small events can become large crises.

Today's event guest is aware of violence not only in urban centres around the world but even in rural areas, be they in Uganda or in the United States. This vast sea of information means that event guests have greater access to information and that the events industry has less ability to hide information. What is still unknown is at what point an excess of information may cause guests simply to shut down and undergo a rejection process. Leisureoriented risk management specialists face the irony that, as information spreads, it increases the potential for violent behaviour. This violence is then reported with the potential of making today's world more dangerous than in any era since the Dark Ages.

Risk managers, then, must deal with an industry that not only is an integral part of many nations' economies, but also plays a major role in the disbursement of information. It is an industry that produces and is produced by information, an industry that sells reality and education, while creating its own postmodern realities based on simulata and plausible facts. In such a diverse industry as the events industry, it is not surprising that there is no one single unifying theory of event risk management. This is a multifaceted industry that has yet to be defined:

Are event attendees the product or the consumers of the product? Is the industry composed of tangibles or is it an intangible many-headed hydra that no one can quite tame? The events industry encompasses such diverse individuals as business travellers, people passing through a locale, people visiting family and friends, delegates to conferences and conventions, audience members, and pleasure seekers. Many event professionals, however, tend to divide the industry into two broad groupings: movement for pleasure and movement for work.

Vacations or leisure events traditionally have been a means by which people attempted to escape from the stress and rigors of everyday life. What once served, however, as a way to repair body and soul has now become a new area for victimisation, and that victimisation often forms the basis of the job of the risk manager in the prevention of crises. The perception that pleasure travel to a particular location may result in the visitor's bodily harm, loss of property, or even death can destroy that locale's tourism industry or the reputation of an event.

Riots at rock concerts and European football (soccer) matches, highly publicised acts of crime in Mexico, terrorist acts against tourists in Egypt, Yemen, and East Africa have all caused a major loss in revenue. These risks turned into reality serve to remind travel/visitor officials of just how sensitive their industry is to security issues. These "crises" often force two components of a nation's society, the travel/events industry and the security industry, to interact with each other and to learn just how interdependent they are on one another. Questions of violence directly impact these industries' ability to promote a safe and worry-free experience.

Vacationers, viewing their trips as an escape from their personal problems and those of the world, tend to assume that they are safe from crime, disease, and even natural calamities. Business travellers, being more cognisant of safety issues, may also shy away from high-risk locales. Although no locale can provide a perfect security/safety environment, an understanding of some of the sociological theoretical models under which visitors operate can help the student of event risk management to prepare for, deal with, and recover from moments of crises.

An unlimited wealth of data demonstrates that the travel and events industries cannot tolerate an environment that is perceived to be unstable. City, county, state/provincial, and national law enforcement agencies play a vital role in making tourists and event attendees feel safe. Convention and visitor bureaus (CVBs), resort hotels, convention organisers, and event planners are aware that a pleasure visitor need not come to their particular community, conference, or event, and therefore see any attack against the safety or security of their guests to be an attack against the essence of their industry.

For example, high crime rates, especially at night, do more than just keep visitors and locals alike from frequenting downtown establishments. These crime rates produce a sociological cancerous blight that in the end gnaws away not only at the tourism industry, but at the chance for holding a particular event, eventually destroying it from the inside. To make matters even more difficult for the event risk management professional, many security forces have only a superficial knowledge of event tourism and travel practices and theory.

Few police departments are cognisant that, taken together, the travel and events industry is the world's largest industry or of the relationship between travel and their own community's economic well-being. There are several exceptions to this rule. To illustrate this point, let us examine one city, Anaheim, California. Anaheim has created a special police unit, called Tourism Oriented Policing Services (TOPS), to deal with almost every travel, meeting, and/or convention problem imaginable.

A special Anaheim police unit now works with Disneyland and its convention centre, focusing on the unique risks involved with conventions and travel. Some of the risks that this unit has learned to handle are risks to non-English-speaking guests, robberies at local hotels, specific crimes targeted at the convention market (such as the stealing of laptop computers), and the special risks that take place in valet companies serving the events industry. In other words, tourismoriented policing is not just crime fighting but also understanding the risks that event-goers face and developing ways to manage those risks.

Police and other security personnel are often geared to the ideal of "to protect" rather than the marketing ideal of "to serve." The TOPS philosophy changes this equation and declares success not as "How many crimes did we solve?" but rather as "How many risks did we identify and how many crimes did we therefore prevent?" TOPS hopes to change the role of law enforcement agencies by helping them to understand how the events industry impacts a community: what its role is in gaining often needed foreign currency, creating employment opportunities, or improving a community's public image and perception of itself.

Additionally, many of the attributes that attract visitors to a community also add to that community's uniqueness and quality of life. Because tourism and events are nontangible products-a "feeling" rather than a "thing"-risk management is dependent not only on concrete plans but also on attitudes held by both the risk management professional and the public. Xenophobic attitudes or simply a "take the guest for granted attitude" are felt by the industry's clients who react negatively to such attitudes, be that person an employee or simply a citizen of the locale being visited.

The risk management professional's attitude is therefore a critical element to his or her success. If these professionals resent their guests and view them as intruders, then no amount of fancy marketing will undo the economic damage done to that community's tourism or events industry. If, on the other hand, these professionals work with visitors with a "cheerful countenance," then the industry creates the synergy necessary to ease it through periods of crisis. Because risk management, from the guest's perspective, touches so many aspects of his or her life away from home, the potential for a crisis is ever present.

Danger can occur not only at the event itself, but also in restaurants and places of entertainment that are in close proximity to an event site, hotels, and transportation arteries. This lack of definition means that event risk management, in its broadest scope, like the industry itself, is undefined. Like a one-cell animal, risk management grows, splits, and travels throughout the social system. Just as there is no one standard and universally accepted definition for the words "tourist" and "tourism," in a like manner there is no one definition of risk management. Working with a composite industry made up of many subindustries, risk managers must deal with crises that are often like the Russian nesting dolls: crises within crises within crises.

Sociological Theories and Event Risk Management

Due, then, to this interlocking of industries within tourism/ meetings and events, one useful method of understanding the role of risk management in crisis prevention is to return to classical sociological theories such as functionalism. Functionalists understand the social system as a series of interlocking components. They assume that a change in any one component of a social system will produce changes throughout the system. From the perspective of event risk management, then, a problem/crisis in any one part of the industry is bound to create problems for that locale's entire industry. Due to this interlocking, functionalists do not distinguish safety issues from security issues.

Functionalists argue instead that any problem that touches upon the well-being of the guest (and therefore the locale's industry as a whole) is one and the same, and any distinction between these two sides of the same coin is mere academic sophistry. For example, let us return to our wedding. How are things interconnected? What happens if the wrong meal is served? What risks are there if a person is seated next to someone with whom he or she is having a quarrel? What crises can take place if a relative, parent, or friend has a bit too much to drink? What happens if the band is too loud, the flowers wilt, or an airplane arrives late? In each of these cases, we can easily see how a change in one aspect of the wedding can cause major problems for other parts of the wedding's social system.

Functionalists argue that, from the perspective of the tourist, a safety issue and a security issue are interchangeable. The functionalist perspective is an important tool in our understanding of the interlinkage of tourism components. What functionalists fail to measure, however, is the intensity of the crisis. Are all crises the same? If not, how does a risk manager decide how to prioritise his or her efforts? Do risks generate "time lags" so that there is a measurable amount of time from one risk to another?

Must the risk manager react to all of the system's components in every crisis? Thus, while functionalist theory sends up a red flag and warns the risk manager that the potential for a crisis is developing, it fails to provide an accurate forecast about the crisis's severity. Functionalism cannot tell the risk manager what parts of the system will be most affected and what the crisis's time frame is or who in a particular crisis may come out to be the winner or the loser. Thus, a murder in a hotel may also affect restaurant business, but the tourism scholar does not know how deep the effect will be or how long it will take to become a crisis.

A second classical way of looking at a tourism risk management system is through conflict theory. Conflict theorists assume that any social system or component-driven industry has a high potential for conflict/competition, not only between locales but also within locales. For example, a city wants to bring in more conventions. A number of businesses, hotels, restaurants, and nightspots, would be highly supportive of such a decision. Nevertheless, opposition arises from locals who fear greater competition for parking space, higher road usage, and an increasing number of social problems. In such a scenario, the events industry might find itself

in direct competition with any number of coalitions that band together to limit the number of conventions brought into the city. In conflict theory, there are always winners and losers and tourism/events are seen as a "zero-sum game." From this perspective, locations and events compete for space, publicity, and clientele. This competition, in turn, is one of the reasons for the business life cycle. Thus, a tourism or event crisis in one part of the world may be seen as an opportunity in another part of the world.

In such a Darwinian worldview, crises are merely shakedowns in which the best and fittest survive to the benefit of the consumer. Risk from this perspective is almost a sport in which managers compete to determine who can best manage the most risks. If we view our wedding from the perspective of conflict theory, we can note a number of risks. It can be argued that the people planning the wedding are as much risk managers, trying to head off potential conflicts, as they are wedding planners. How many of us have been to a family wedding where the bride and groom's side may already be in conflict, or where one or more of the couple's parents are divorced and not speaking to each other? How popular is the photographer with the guests? How often do waiters and waitresses lose their tempers?

From this perspective, weddings are like golf, the lower the score, the better the game is played. Such competition, however, does not necessarily signify the best tourism product. The history of consumer products has shown that survival may not be based on quality of product but rather on quality of marketing, timing, or symbiotic name recognition. Tourism crises may cause a shakedown in the tourism market and produce strong marketing agencies, but these crises do not necessarily translate into a better tourism product or a better managed event. The prism of symbolic interaction is another way by which to analyse a tourism crisis.

Over the years, this perspective, as first understood by the sociologist Max Weber, has evolved into postmodernism and then into iconic theory. Scholars who accept this form of theoretical paradigm argue that tourism, meetings, or special events are highly sensitive to image creation. The basis for their academic argument is that these industries sell memories and are "image" producers. The meetings and events industry, for those who work in symbolic interaction, is about the packaging of a collective memory and associating it with (a) specific place(s) in time or space. From the symbolic interaction perspective, crises are interpreted in a symbolic and symbiotic manner. An example of this symbolism is in the presence or nonpresence of a police/security force at an event site.

In many event venues, a police/security presence may serve the industry as a "psychological" security blanket and a way to avoid crises. Visitors report that they feel more comfortable when they know that an area is well patrolled. In contrast, however, too many police officers in a particular location may send the message that there is a good reason to be afraid, that the officers are there as a result of a crisis, or that the area is dangerous. Because most people connect a uniformed officer to a range of meanings, the tourism centre that chooses to have a security force present must create a setting in which these security personnel symbolise hospitality rather than restraint, service over protection, and security over threat.

When security departments produce negative images, they can become part of the risk crisis. For example, negative media reports about Los Angeles and Mexico City have added additional challenges to the tourism industries in those cities. The recent example of New York City police officers doing nothing while more than fifty women were molested in Central Park during the Puerto Rico Day parade has been reported throughout the world. In that case, due to poor risk management and assessment, a major crisis developed for both the city's tourism community and its police force. The opposite can also be true. In some communities, local security forces have succeeded in becoming symbolic icons, representing not just the use of force but also a cultural attraction. In those cases, the police force is not only a deterrent to crime but also an important icon of that society.

You, as an event risk manager, must be aware of the following:

1. Events are a volunteeristic activity. As such, the industry must resell itself on a consistent basis. The theoretical consequences of this proposition are many. For example:
   a. Guests need not come to a particular place or return to that place. An event, then, always involves a sense of marketing. To survive, the professional must assume that brand loyalty or even desire to buy can never be taken for granted.
   b. Most guests expect a safe and secure environment. The one exception to this rule is the allocentric adventure market where people seek danger. For example, consider the rise of storm chasers or those who specifically choose to visit a war zone. Even among highly allocentric travellers, danger can be divided into expected dangers (i.e., dangers factored into the trip) and random violence (i.e.,

dangers that are produced in a violent manner and not considered part of the experience). The large majority of guests, however, assume that a place is safe and secure.

2. Most guests do not distinguish between the concepts of safety and security. The poisoning of food and an act of terrorism often have the same consequences. This dedifferentiation between the terms again holds a number of consequences for the industry. For example:
   a. The farther the person is from a crisis, the worse that crisis seems and the longer the crisis lasts in the outsider's memory.
   b. Guests tend to be more ignorant of local conditions than those who live in a locale. Thus, fear and rumor have greater consequences than does reality. Facts are those that seem plausible rather than those that are empirically provable.
   c. Potential visitors are often highly unsophisticated when it comes to geography. Due to geographic ignorance, fear, and media hype, a crisis in one part of a nation may affect that entire nation's tourism and even tourism throughout that region. For example, consider the drop in event attendance and general tourism throughout the eastern Mediterranean during NATO's Kosovo action.
   d. Event guests do not distinguish between one part of an industry and another. Thus, if a crisis occurs in a locale's food-handling sector, the negative publicity may produce fallout in that locale's lodging industry, attractions, and so forth. Other than a few worldwide attractions, such as the Eiffel Tower and the Taj Mahal, most tourists, especially on first visits, come to a locale and not to a site.

3. There is no one formula to describe all guests. What may be a crisis for one person may not be a crisis for another person. Classical psychographic tourism theory tends to divide visitors along various continuums. For example, we can adapt the Plog model to event risk management and divide guests along the allocentric-psychographic continuum. This typology shows the amount of risk that a person is willing to take. Another typology is that of the inner- and outerdirected event guest. In this continuum, guests are situated according to their motivations to attend an event: Did they attend this event to impress others or merely to please themselves? In all cases, the term special events covers a number of people who view different events as indications of a crisis or lack of crisis. Table 1 distinguishes allocentric from psychocentric event participants.

Table 1. Allocentric and Psychocentric Event Participants

Allocentric Event Guest	Psychocentric Event Guest
Rock concert guest	Theater attendee
Ropes course participant	Conference participant
White-water rafter	Visitor to a museum

During the last century, all forms of event participation have grown from an activity of the well-to-do to a part of everyday life. Leisure, parasitic in nature, was once the idle time of the rich. In the mid-twentieth century, leisure became a product for the working person, and once it became producible en masse, it became an integral part of local economies. There are several other theoretical models that can be of use to the event risk manager. The event risk manager must prevent the risk by:

— *Staging the product*: It means that the "tourism product's safety" must be organised in such a way that it achieves its aims for both the consumer (visitor) and the supplier.

— *Arranging the product*: Risk management must stand out within its geographical or psychological environment.

— *Contextualising the product*: Risk management needs to be placed within, or purposely removed from, the context of itself, be that context physical, historical, or psychological.

— *Thematising the product*

— *Authenticising the product*: An event crisis is any event in which the visitor does not receive his or her "paid-for reality" for whatever reason. If the product does not deliver a heightened experience (even if the heightened experience is rest and relaxation) into which the client can be fully immersed, then the potential for a crisis develops.

Therefore, it may be concluded that there is no one single definition of a tourism/event crisis. As such, the range of solutions to these crises is as complex as the crises themselves. Following is a potpourri of examples of how different crises have been confronted. The list is not meant to be exhaustive, but rather a snapshot of different event scenarios. Perhaps the greatest crisis that event management can encounter is the loss of life. Be this loss from kidnapping at a diving resort in Southeast Asia or a serial killer stalking the streets of a large urban centre, no destination or venue can long survive capricious and random acts of violence. To combat this threat, event security specialists have developed techniques such as:

— Interacting with guests as an implicit anticrime tool. Even in cities with high crime rates, crime tends to be highly concentrated in small geographic regions. Security specialists can instruct tourists on the safest routes between attractions. These interactions, however, require highly trained security professionals in tourism and tourism safety/security.

— Developing, in conjunction with local tourism offices/bureaus and event organisers, plans to deal with event guests who are victimised by crime. Tourism theory predicts that kind words and caring after a crime has occurred can (but do not always) mitigate some of the crime's negative effects. A security officer's professionalism can create a situation where the victimised tourist leaves with a positive, or at least less negative, attitude about the locale's hospitality rather than as a vocal critic.

— Becoming ambassadors of goodwill for their product. Police and security departments may wish to consider the adoption of special uniforms that match their city's image. Such uniquely tailored uniforms remind local townspeople that their police department/security force not only serves and protects them, but has also adopted a proactive stance in helping to bring economic benefit to the community. Not all crises are of a violent nature. As the range of tourism crises to manage is exhaustive, following are some other techniques that have been used:

— Developing interesting jobs and creating high morale. By creating interesting and well-paying jobs, the community's stake in its local tourism industry increases. As such, when crises do happen, the entire community pulls together to help mitigate and rebuild from the crises.

— Improving the quality of life. Typically, tourists and event guests visit communities with sound ecologies, good restaurants, and a multitude of attractions. These same considerations are important factors in determining a community's quality of life. By creating an atmosphere that visitors enjoy, tourism/travel officials encourage leaders in both the public and the private sectors to further improve the community's quality-of-life aspects.

— Being open and honest. When a crisis occurs, the last thing the tourism industry can afford is to lie. Facts about the crisis should be given to the media in a nondefensive and forthright manner. Specific people should be designated as representatives who can provide the media with clear and precise facts.

From a tourism/travel perspective, crises have certain common patterns and "life cycles." Accordingly, the risk manager should take into account the following:

— Determining what preparations are already in place and what resources are available.

— Involving the local population in the disaster. Is there special attention that can be given by the locals to the survivors?

— Considering the postdisaster healing process.

— Knowing that no place is immune. The worst possible mindframe is for you to believe that no form of disaster can occur at your locale. For example, the random shootings of tourists that have taken place in the United States are exactly that, random. So far, there has been no pattern determined as to type of place, type of perpetrator, or type of victim.

Being prepared for a worst case scenario. In any disaster, there will be a threat of personal injury and death. Disasters mean that there will be disruption of operations, financial strain on the tourism locale or company, and damage to the tourism/travel company's image. Prior to an event, take the time to plan two or three scenarios. Tourism/travel professionals should be able to answer such questions as: What actions would you take during a disruption?

> Do the people in your community, or at your tourism locale, have adequate insurance to survive a disaster? Will employees and their families have adequate finances to avoid financial ruin? Does the locale have two or three generic recovery marketing plans set to go should a disaster strike?

In all disasters be prepared for disaster fallout. This fallout can occur both during and after a disaster and can include such things as adverse media coverage, constant involvement and monitoring by outside sources, negative name brand association, damage to destination/resort's image, lowering of staff morale, and anger on the part of the victims toward their hosts.

Project Management Systems

Using a project management system will help you establish a systematic approach to all events. The project management system provides you with a superstructure to enable you to systematically approach every event using the same framework. Many events—especially those in the social market-are driven by emotional decisions rather than systematic or logical approaches. The project management system will depersonalise the event as it provides you with an objective process for reviewing the event development.

Communication is critical throughout the Event Management process, and the project management system will help you facilitate clear communications with stakeholders from many different fields. Through meetings and documents, project management provides a transparent system to promote better communications. Many corporate and government organisations already utilise project management systems; therefore, using this system will help you conform to those that are already in place in your clients' organisations.

Accountability is increasingly one of the more important outcomes of any event project. The project management system helps ensure accountability through the continuous outputs that are required to update the progress of the event. O'Toole and Mikolaitis believe that, through the adoption of project management systems, you will be able to increase the visibility for the profession of Event Leadership. If your work is often invisible until the actual start of the event, the project management system will provide a continuous flow of information charting the progress of the event as it develops and will provide your client and others with an overview of the complexity of your job.

Training is critical for your staff and volunteers and, by providing them with a project management system to follow, this training may be simplified and expedited. The project management system will put your staff and volunteers to work at a quicker pace and will motivate them to consistently perform better over the life span of the event. In addition to facilitating training, project management competency helps develop transferable skills that will help you attract the best people. As a result of working within your project management system, your staff and volunteers will learn a system that may be transferred and applied to a seemingly infinite number of jobs and careers. Finally, as an event project manager you will establish a diverse body of knowledge that may be transmitted to other organisations.

In addition, you will be able to accumulate and refine the knowledge you receive from specific events and related projects from around the world. Whether it is a moon landing mission by NASA or the development and deployment of the new Transportation Security Administration (TSA), you can benefit from the successful project management experiences of other organisations. In traditional project management, a technique entitled the

Project Breakdown Structure (PBS) is often used to establish the organisational structure.

Similar to the traditional organisational chart, the PBS provides a thorough overview of all of the event requirements. After the event has been thoroughly defined, the work that will be required must be carefully analysed. During this decomposition period, the work that will be conducted for the event is broken down into smaller units of work entitled tasks. Tasks or activities are generally singular, independent entities that may be individually managed. They also have specific start and finish times. Finally, they require clearly assigned resources (labour, finance, time). When several tasks are bundled together, they form a work package.

When an important task is accomplished, project managers refer to this stage as a milestone or the completion of an important task. Scheduling is perhaps one of the most valuable advantages of using a project management system for your event. Tasks are usually divided into two types of scheduling systems. Parallel scheduling refers to tasks that may be performed at the same time. Serial scheduling refers to tasks that must be performed in a sequence, such as when the lighting company must first hang the lights before the rental company places the tables and chairs for a banquet.

Timelines for your events may benefit from a pictorial tool which demonstrates the major tasks that need to be accomplished. Creating and documenting the critical tasks and critical path are major responsibilities for the event project manager. The ability of the event project manager to list, prioritise, and sequence the tasks will ultimately determine the overall success of the event from an operational and financial standpoint. Influence diagrams and sensitivity analyses are used to mitigate future challenges.

The influence diagram is a chart that demonstrates through boxes and arrows what tasks are interdependent on others. Most importantly, it clearly demonstrates that events are part of larger systems and one change in the system can affect hundreds of other components in the event. The sensitivity analysis is the identification of the degree of influence any part of the event has on the entire event as a whole. This analysis also aids in the risk-management controls for the event because it demonstrates how a small change in one area can affect other areas of the entire event. Event Leaders will greatly benefit from project management training.

Importance of Effective Communication

Event management is a profession whose success or failure ratio often depends on people's ability to communicate effectively with one another. It does not matter whether this communication is oral, written, electronic, or all three. What is important is that Event Managers become practiced communicators in order to maintain clear communications with all stakeholders. Regardless of the communication channel that you are using, you want to make sure that you make your point clearly and establish the right priorities in your message.

Often, both visual and auditory noise will provide a barrier to open communication. Visual noise includes those visual distractions that take place when you are trying to communicate with others. Auditory noise may be music, traffic, or other distractions that interfere with others' ability to hear and concentrate on what you are saying. Remove all noise before trying to communicate with others. Find a quiet place to meet, remove visual distractions, and verify and confirm that those you are communicating with comprehend what you are sharing. Written communications are essential not only for record keeping but also for purposes of mass distribution.

It is impossible to transmit verbally to 1000 people an event update without distortion. Use memorandums, briefing statements, bulletins, and other documents to communicate effectively to one or many others. Memoranda should include an "Action Required" statement to inform the reader how best to respond and in what time frame. Bulletins must be sporadic, or you run the risk of becoming the person who cried "wolf" once too often and now is ignored by everyone. Newsletters are a particularly effective tool for communications; however, use caution, as they are extremely labour intensive. Perhaps one of the best ways to communicate is through a meeting.

When scheduling a meeting, make certain that you prepare an agenda in advance that lists the items for discussion. Distribute this document in advance of the meeting to those who will attend and ask them to comment. This will help them prepare for the meeting. Use the agenda to guide the meeting and, as the leader, serve as a facilitator for discussion. Using a flipchart will help you capture ideas while sticking to the agenda. One extremely effective device is to assign the meeting participants prework so that they come to the meeting prepared and ready to make specific contributions.

Make sure that your meeting does not take much longer than initially planned; otherwise, you will give the impression of being a disorganised person who does not value your own time and the time that others will invest in the meeting. Alternative communication techniques include producing audiotapes and videotapes as well as using teleconferencing through compressed video (telephone lines). Since the average person commutes 20 or more minutes twice daily to the office, this is an excellent time to put your meeting or information on audiotape, add a little music, and share your ideas.

The major drawback to this alternative is that the communication is one-way. Videotapes also allow you to express your thoughts creatively with photos, interviews, and music and to show the tape before a large group of people creating excitement in numbers. Two-way video using existing telephone lines and a compressed system is an effective way to present data, visuals, and some person-to-person interaction.

It is also relatively inexpensive compared to traditional satellite uplink/downlink technology. The use of computer online chat rooms has grown in popularity due to the rapid expansion of the Internet technologies. When using chat rooms, avoid personal issues and conduct postings in a businesslike manner. Personal issues may be addressed through other mediums, such as telephone calls. Chat rooms are excellent information-exchange opportunities, and you will find that your colleagues will provide you with new resources for producing better events.

Consideration of External Factors of Events

Event operations planning and impact analysis activities that address the core factors affecting planned special event severity. That is, travel demand, road/site capacity, and event operation. A number of secondary factors warrant consideration in the event operations phase, including:

— Available resources

— Weather

— Concurrent roadway construction

— Concurrent planned special events

These factors can greatly influence the level of impact a planned special event has on transportation system operations. By gaining an understanding of the special challenges that these external factors present, the event planning team can develop appropriate contingency response plans, using the tools and strategies.

An assessment of the level of impact that an external factor has on travel during a particular planned special event involves the consideration of the following components:

— *Duration* - temporal impact (e.g., when does the external factor impact operations and for how long?).

— *Extent* - spatial impact or scope of area affected (e.g., does the external factor impact a particular corridor or the entire region?)

— *Intensity* - volume of impact (e.g., how severe is the impact?)

Practitioners should express the impact of an external factor in terms of how it affects travel demand, road/site capacity, and personnel/equipment resource quantities. Feasibility study input data can reflect adjustments made due to certain anticipated external factors, or practitioners can rerun parking and roadway capacity analyses to account for a new unexpected factor (e.g., occurrence of emergency road construction). In turn, revised results may warrant adjustments to the event traffic management plan.

Available Resources

Available resources refer to the quantity and experience of personnel and equipment available to plan and conduct day-of-event travel management operations. Besides the size of a planned special event, the level of required resources depend on time/place of occurrence, other planned special events, and equipment status. A special factor that may place significant strain on available resources involves the occurrence of planned special events at a venue under reconstruction. Stakeholder response to on-site parking restrictions include redevelopment of traffic management plans to accommodate parking demand, pedestrian access, and traffic flow in the immediate vicinity of the venue.

Weather Conditions

Weather conditions affect travel demand, road/site capacity, or both. For example, in winter, snow banks in permanent venue parking areas reduce the number of on-site parking spaces required for an event sell-out. Rain can create significant problems for unpaved parking areas and access roads. A one-day rain event totalling approximately 0.70 inches during the 2002 U.S. Golf Open forced the traffic management team to close all unpaved parking areas adjacent to the golf course. With regard to travel demand, weather conditions have a significant impact on attendance and/or the rate of arrivals and departures at some special events. For instance, event patrons will attend an event at a domed stadium on a rainy day, but patrons will bypass arriving at the venue early to tailgate, thus concentrating patron arrivals.

Concurrent Road Construction and Special Events

The occurrence of planned events, including road construction and other planned special events, create a range of impacts affecting different traffic management plan components. On a regional level, the characteristics of concurrent planned events reduce available capacity in roadway corridors serving a particular planned special event, thus affecting traffic flow patterns. Local impacts include reduced parking supply, in the event of other area planned special events, and restricted traffic circulation. The identification of concurrent planned events requires interagency communication at the local, county, and state level.

Evaluation of Events

The event leadership process, as shown in Figure 2, is a dynamic spiral that is literally without end.

The first phase-research-is connected with the last-evaluation. In this phase, you will ask: "What is it we wish to evaluate, and how will we best accomplish this?" Events may be evaluated by each part of the Event Management process or through a general comprehensive review of all phases. It is up to you and your stakeholders to decide what information you require to improve your planning and then implement effective strategies to accomplish this phase. Perhaps the most common form of event evaluation is the written survey.

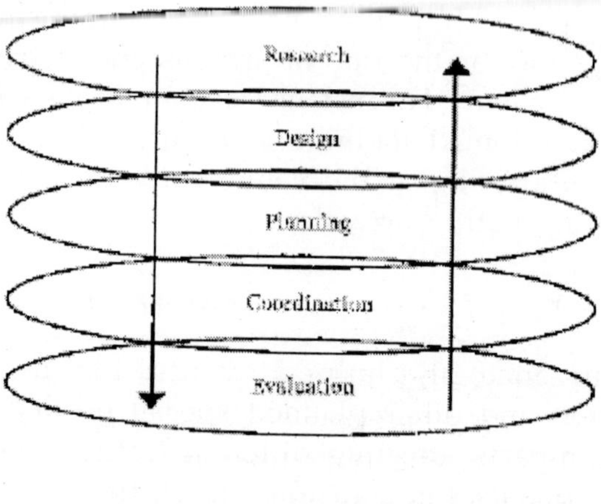

Figure 2. Event Management Process

Usually, the survey is conducted immediately following the event, to collect the satisfaction level of the participants and spectators. As with any evaluation method, there are pros and cons to immediate feedback. One bias is the immediate nature of the feedback, which prohibits a respondent from digesting the total event experience before providing his or her feedback.

Another form of evaluation is the use of monitors. A monitor is a trained person who will observe an element of the event and provide both written and verbal feedback to the Event Manager. The event monitor usually has a checklist or survey to complete and will then offer additional comments as required. The benefit of this type of evaluation is that it permits a trained, experienced event staff member or volunteer to observe the event objectively while it is taking place and provide instructive comments.

The third form of event evaluation is the telephone or mail survey conducted after the event. In this evaluation, the Event Manager surveys the spectators and participants after the event through either a mail or a telephone survey. By waiting a few days after the event to collect these data, the Event Manager is able to glean from the respondents how their attitudes have changed and developed after some time has passed since participating in the event. A new form of evaluation that is growing in popularity is the pre- and post-event survey. This evaluation allows an Event Manager to determine the respondents' knowledge, opinions, and other important information both before and after their attendance at an event.

This is especially helpful when trying to match expectations to reality. For example, an event guest may state upon entering an event that he or she expects, based on the advertising and public relations, to enjoy nonstop entertainment. However, upon completing the exit interview, the guest registers disappointment because of the gaps in the programming. This type of evaluation helps event organisers close gaps between overpromising and underdelivering certain aspects of an event. Registration mail-in rebates and other incentives may be offered for filling out both surveys. Regardless of the form of evaluation you use, it is critical that you not wait until the end of the event to find out how you are doing.

Take the temperature of your guests hourly to make certain that you are on target in meeting your goals and objectives. By doing this, you are able to reset your course immediately and ensure that, together, you will arrive at the same destination-a successful event. This Event Management process is the conceptual framework for every effective event. The process is dynamic and will require selectivity by the Event Manager to determine where to begin and how to proceed to best accomplish the objectives.

One event may be past the research stage and the Event Manager retained merely to coordinate the elements. Still another may be midway through the planning phase. The effective Event Manager will immediately recognise that the event process cannot be complete or totally effective unless each phase is considered carefully. It matters not where you begin the process. It is essential that every phase be considered, visited, and understood.

BIBLIOGRAPHY

Boggs, R., "Challenges in Supporting Planned Special Events in Your Community," *Presented at the Institute of Transportation Engineers 2003 Technical Conference and Exhibit Program,*" Fort Lauderdale, Florida, March 23–26, 2003.

Carson, J.L. and R.G. Bylsma, *Transportation Planning and Management for Special Events,* NCHRP Synthesis 309, Transportation Research Board, National Research Council, Washington D.C., 2003.

Corbin, J., "Strategies to Improve Management of Travel for All Planned Special Events in a Region," *Presented at the 82nd Annual Meeting of the Transportation Research Board,* Washington, D.C., January 12–16, 2003.

Jacobson, L., *Highway Traffic Operations and Freeway Management State-of-the-Practice White Paper,* Report No. FHWA-OP-03-076, Federal Highway Administration, Washington, D.C., March 2003.

Kelleher, B., "Action on the Highways," *Transportation News,* Florida Department of Transportation, Vol. 36, No. 1, January 2003.

Laitner, B., "Royal Oak Preparing to Handle Crowds of Red Wings Fans," *Detroit Free Press,* June 13, 2002.

Montag, D.A., *Trip Generation Rates and Characteristics for Theme-Oriented Fairs and Festivals,* West Virginia University, Morgantown, West Virginia, May 1998.

Sattayhatewa, P. and R.L. Smith, "Development of Parking Choice Models for Special Events," *Presented at the 82nd*

Annual Meeting of the Transportation Research Board, Washington, D.C., January 12–16, 2003.

Schmitt, B., "State Troopers Close Roads into Downtown Detroit," *Detroit Free Press*, June 13, 2002.

Shaw, T., *Performance Measures of Operational Effectiveness for Highway Segments and Systems*, NCHRP Synthesis 311, Transportation Research Board, National Research Council, Washington D.C., 2003.

Smith, M.C., "King of Super Bowl Roads," *Orange County Register*, January 25, 2003.

Traffic Considerations for Special Events, Institute of Transportation Engineers, Washington, D.C., 1976, 44 pp.

Volz, M.A. and B.J. Nicholson, "Kansas Speedway Event Management Using ITS," n.d.

Womble, J.E., "A Transportation and Tourism Profile of Visitors to the 1984 Louisiana World Exposition in New Orleans," *ITE Journal*, Vol. 55, No. 4, April 1985, pp. 49–53.

INDEX